The

big book

of team
motivating
games

*Spirit-Building, Problem-Solving,
and Communication Games for Every Group*

Mary Scannell & Edward E. Scannell

New York Chicago San Francisco Lisbon London Madrid Mexico City
Milan New Delhi San Juan Seoul Singapore Sydney Toronto

Library of Congress Cataloging-in-Publication Data

Scannell, Mary, 1959–
    The big book of team-motivating games : spirit-building, problem-solving, and
communication games for every group / Mary Scannell and Edward Scannell.
        p.   cm.
    ISBN 978-0-07-162962-1 (alk. paper)
    1. Teams in the workplace.   2. Management games.   3. Employee
motivation.   I. Scannell, Edward E.   II. Title.

HD66.S33   2009
658.4′022—dc22   2009027428

5 6 7 8 9 10 11 12 13 14 15 16 17 18 19 20 21 22   DOC/DOC   1 5 4 3 2

ISBN   978-0-07-162962-1
MHID   0-07-162962-9

Interior design by Think Book Works
Illustrations by Drake Carr and Jaclyn LaBarbera

McGraw-Hill books are available at special quantity discounts to use as premiums and
sales promotions or for use in corporate training programs. To contact a representative,
please e-mail us at bulksales@mcgraw-hill.com.

Contents

Acknowledgments

Thank you to all the teams I've worked with over the years. Your participation, enthusiasm, and feedback have provided me with valuable insight. Thanks for playing.

Thank you to the incredible trainers out there for sharing the best practices in this field. I have learned so much from you. Thanks for your generosity in practice and spirit.

Thank you to my home team—my family, whom I would choose to have on my team any day, and my friends, who demonstrate that listening is a key component of communication. Thanks for your support and encouragement.

—Mary Scannell

Since the first book in the *Games Trainers Play* series some 25 years ago, we have been lucky enough to see overall sales of that book and its successors (*More Games Trainers Play, Still More Games Trainers Play*, etc.) exceed one million copies. For this, we are indebted to the thousands of friends and colleagues who have attended our workshops and seminars with such groups as National Speakers Association (NSA), Meeting Professionals International (MPI), and American Society for Training and Development (ASTD). Coupled with our human resources departments (HRD) and human resources management (HRM) groups across the globe from Africa to New Zealand, these audiences have helped us field-test the activities and exercises in this book.

A special thanks goes to Dr. John Newstrom, the original coauthor for all of the previous *Games* books. We initially met as fellow faculty members at Arizona State University's College of Business some 30 years ago, and this working relationship has turned into a long-standing friendship.

Thank you to Cathie LaBarbera and Mike Scannell for their help and dedication throughout this process. Finally, a note of thanks goes to Emily Carleton, our editor at McGraw-Hill, who first approached us a few months back and asked us to consider another *Games* book. This book developed through her request and continued guidance.

—Edward E. Scannell, CMP, CSP

Introduction

Coming together is a beginning. Keeping together is progress. Working together is success.

—Henry Ford

Team Building

The importance of team motivation has been well documented over the past several years. Team-building exercises create connections and harmony in the workplace and help ensure that we can work both more productively and more effectively.

There are two different types of team building: (1) a traditional classroom approach, which is appropriate for strategic planning sessions, and (2) a more experiential approach, which may involve the participants in some type of outdoor activity. With either approach, the goal is to get the team members to stretch their comfort zones in a supportive, encouraging environment, which is a great way to allow the team to learn and grow.

A major reason a company may choose to organize team-building activities is to allow colleagues to interact in a more informal atmosphere. This informal atmosphere builds deeper relationships than would the usual workplace setting. These deeper relationships help colleagues interact more effectively once they return to their jobs.

With the constant changes in the workforce, it benefits both seasoned and new employees to learn to work together more effectively. For example, a Gen Xer and a more senior manager bring different values and belief systems to the job. By engaging in team-motivating activities, the individuals may become more accepting and understanding of the perspectives and experiences of others. Team building has proven successful in changing behavior, ultimately making for a more cohesive and trusting team. Even if some are resistant to take part in the "fun and games," they can still benefit and learn new concepts to use in their everyday interactions with coworkers. In fact, it is often the case that the more resistant the participant, the more dramatic the result.

In choosing an appropriate activity, it is important for the facilitator to identify the goal or purpose of the exercise. If an outdoor activity is selected, make sure adequate space is available. Consider the profile of the group: age, gender, whether they already know one another, and so on. For outdoor activities, the physical condition and fitness of the participants must also be considered.

Several factors impact the overall effectiveness of any team. Communication skills are critical and can often make or break an otherwise effective team. Creativity and problem-solving abilities frequently come into play, as well as interpersonal skills such as developing rapport and trust. Discovering that one person's actions can influence the effectiveness of the entire team is a great learning experience.

The role of the facilitator is important, with three skills necessary to this task:

1. Keen observation skills, to provide insight to the team during the debrief discussion
2. The ability to ask thought-provoking questions, to maximize the lessons of the activity
3. The ability to fully involve everyone in the discussion, to build confidence and collaboration

If the company management wants effective teams, they must get involved in the process. (Team motivation is not a spectator sport!) Then after the program, it is imperative that supervisors and managers continue to be supportive and refresh the camaraderie displayed during the activity.

Teams

The old acronym *TEAM*, "Together everyone accomplishes more," is as true today as it ever was. In today's competitive work environment, most employees are involved in one or more teams. The team approach to productivity has become the standard. In one recent study, managers were asked to identify the most important traits of the perfect staff member. Being a team player was the number one factor, outranking such qualities as experience, problem-solving, dedication, and communication skills. Without question, the use of teams has increased, and good team players are critical to the success of any organization.

Leadership

Those in leadership roles can do their part by providing a supportive environment and encouraging team members to identify with their team. To maintain this level of unity, leaders should allow time for regular team meetings and actively demonstrate their belief in the importance of the team's contributions. They can also encourage continuing professional development and education for their employees, assuring them of the organization's commitment to the advancement of their careers. To help the team excel, leaders need to provide clear objectives and ensure agreement as to the roles each team member is expected to perform. But what matters most is fostering opportunities for team members to connect and interact with one another. The team-motivating games in this book are designed to provide these opportunities.

Motivation

Sustaining motivation within a team, especially during lean or transitional times, can be a challenging endeavor. Team building provides the framework to accomplish this by creating an opportunity for teams to identify a common goal, solve problems, assign responsibility, encourage each other, and integrate their talents to reach their goal.

What It Takes

The most effective teams focus on a common purpose, while demonstrating reliability and cohesion. They operate on a strong foundation of trust and individual commitment to the team. By understanding the sequential stages of the team's formation, team members—including leaders—can better understand the process involved in developing an effective team.

Building Your Team

When creating a new team, many questions need to be asked and answered. For example, "What purpose will this team serve?" "Who will be involved?" "What rules and guidelines do we need?" "Who is responsible for what?" and "How will team decisions be made?" As these questions are answered, teams begin to evolve.

Typically, a team develops through the following process:

The Forming Stage

This is the polite, ice-breaking, "get to know each other" stage, when team members begin to figure out who's who and where everyone fits in the picture. This may take place at the opening meeting or an orientation session. Informal gatherings and discussions after the initial meeting are also part of this stage of group formation. It is important to create an environment that is safe and secure. The team will be looking to the leader for guidance and direction. At this beginning stage, it's essential to get buy-in from all the team members and candidly identify the pros and cons of teamwork and team building. At this stage the team builds its foundation, so spending significant time in this stage will pay off later.

The Storming Stage

In this stage, interpersonal issues may arise—for example, "Who sets our goals?" or "Why was Jack selected for this function?" Members may voice these and a host of other challenges. This stage typically occurs when conflict is introduced into a previously safe and comfortable environment. Many teams experience this in the second week or so, because that's when reality sets in. Things that may not have mattered in the beginning suddenly seem important, and conflict arises as a result. It is critical that these concerns be straightforwardly addressed. Unless interpersonal conflicts and dissonance are handled at this early stage, the success of the team is in jeopardy. Once again, strong leadership is the key to navigating through this stage.

The Norming Stage

Cooperation and trust are now becoming the norm for this team. The team begins to better understand the respective personalities of other team members, so their diverse perspectives can come together to work more effectively. Good things are starting to happen, and as a result the team feels more confident, connected, and creative. The team continues to look to the leader for support during this stage.

The Performing Stage

Here, you're on a roll! The team has momentum and energy, and ideally all team members are willing to contribute equally. This is the most productive of all the stages. Tasks are identified and handled efficiently by designated members of the team. Individuals respect the contributions of others, and the team is well on its way to meeting, and even surpassing, its goals and objectives.

The Transforming Stage

This final stage brings reflection. It is a time for the team to provide feedback and to show appreciation. The team looks to the leader for recognition in this stage.

Team-Motivating Games

The games in this book will help the team navigate through many of the different stages of their development. There are games to help team members get to know each other better, games to encourage open communication, problem-solving initiatives, and even activities that allow team members to show their appreciation for one another. Use these games to take your team from a group of individuals to a high-performing team.

Tell me and I forget. Show me and I may remember. Involve me and I will understand.

—*Chinese proverb*

Why Use Team-Motivating Games?

It has been shown that experiential learning activities and exercises can enhance the interpersonal skills so critical to a team's success. As it turns out, this is true—learning *can* be fun! When participants are engaged in the process, the interactions are not only more enjoyable, but far more productive. There is an expectation on the part of participants that they can take control of their learning by being involved.

- Games help the facilitator *make a point*—one that is clear, memorable, and relevant to the task at hand. Games are powerful tools to drive home key ideas.
- Games help *build morale.* They provide a sharp contrast to "business as usual" by injecting an element of fun and playfulness into team meetings.
- Games help team members learn to *trust each other.* They provide opportunities for sharing insights, emotions, and experiences as the team develops solutions. Increased understanding and appreciation for each other's viewpoints are valuable by-products of the discussions during the activity debrief.
- Games help team members *become more flexible and adaptive.* Members soon understand and appreciate the fact that there may be more than one way to solve a problem.
- Games provide opportunities for team leaders to *reinforce appropriate behaviors*. When cooperation is displayed, when creativity is demonstrated, or when interpersonal barriers begin to break down, a leader can show appreciation for the desirable responses elicited from a team-building game and debrief session.
- Games *provide opportunities to connect.* Plato said it best, "You can discover more about a person in an hour of play than in a year of conversation." When we reach out and connect with our team, it breaks

down barriers. Technology, with all its benefits and conveniences, can be a barrier to human connection.

Characteristics of Team-Motivating Games

The games in this book are appropriate to use in training sessions, team meetings, as well as team-building programs.

Features of these games:

- They are *quick and easy*. The games themselves take little time—some as little as five minutes. The discussion that follows may take longer depending on the purpose of the activity.
- They are *inexpensive*. Very few props are necessary, and many can be used again and again before needing any replacement.
- They are *participative*. The games involve the entire team—no one sits on the sidelines. Games help participants focus their energy and attention, therefore making them think, interact, and have fun—all while learning to be better team players.
- They are *entertaining*. For example, the use of props piques interest and adds realism and variety to the program. The props can be as simple as a ball or a handout.
- They are *low risk*. All the games in this book have been field-tested in a wide variety of sessions with a wide variety of groups and teams. The games are user friendly, and people respond positively to them. When these games are matched with the right content, context, and personnel—and presented in a positive and enthusiastic manner—you can't go wrong.

These games will prove to be effective time and time again.

Your Keys to Success

It's easy to get good players. Getting them to play together is the hard part.

—Casey Stengel

Let Them Figure It Out

At some point during these activities, frustration is inevitable, but remember that working through challenges is a big part of the process. Allow the team to work through it unassisted. This process is key to the experience and the meat of your debrief discussion. One of the most effective things a facilitator can do to enrich the debrief discussion is take notes. If your groups are large, you may find it more effective to let them debrief in smaller teams to encourage more participation. Remember, the facilitator does not have to be a part of every debrief discussion to make it meaningful to the participants. One option is to have discussion questions printed ahead of time on slips of paper to distribute to the teams, so they can lead their own debrief discussion.

Learning without thought is labor lost; thought without learning is perilous.

—Confucius

Keep Your Energy Up!

Energy is contagious. If you are not having fun, there's a good chance your team won't have fun either. Teams tend to look to the leader for cues as to how to react to the day's events. If you don't buy into the activity, they won't either. For you to buy into an activity, it needs to serve a purpose: for example, a learning experience, an opportunity to bond and build trust, a chance to have fun. Whatever it is, figure it out for yourself ahead of time. It will help you create a nourishing and enthusiastic environment. Sincerity can't be faked, so it's time to "get real!"

Be Flexible

Games have rules. But as we all know, rules are made to be bent, broken, or tossed out. Most of these activities can be made more or less challenging with a simple twist of the rules. Be aware of what the team needs, and be flexible enough to adapt the rules to create a rewarding learning environment.

The Facilitator's Role

Your role is to provide the framework. Let the team create the masterpiece—their own unique experience. If issues come up—planned or unplanned—use them as teaching moments. If the team members zig, when you expected them to zag, go with it. Who is to say what is "off course," anyway? Overall, these games will motivate. Monitor the energy level—theirs and yours. Time can be cut or stretched depending on how the game is going and the needs of the team.

The Team Needs What the Team Needs

These activities are revealing. Trust that they will bring out the important dynamics within the team. You may think the team is way off your agenda, but be willing to go with it. Be aware of what's really happening and use it in the debrief discussion.

Failure

If you were searching on the Internet for a quote about how failures point the way and lead to success, you'd get a whole lot of hits. Failure is part of the process. As a facilitator, it can be a challenge to lead the debrief discussion when the team does not accomplish their goal. But keep in mind that for the team, this experience can be a powerful learning tool and can create a memorable experience. Learn to facilitate the good, the bad, and the ugly.

Go Paperless

Many of the activities in this book suggest using paper, but it's really up to you. When you forgo the paper, it forces a team to talk and rely on each other, which builds trust. It's good to be green—for you *and* your team.

Go out and Play

Unless you need a flip chart (and even those can be carted outside), most of these activities can be taken outside for a change of environment. The experience definitely changes when you get out in the fresh air—and it feels even more removed from the office environment. If we ever have the outside option when we facilitate team-building programs, we take it. You may want to do the same.

Common Sense

Some movement is required in some of the games. Invite your participants to use their common sense. If an activity is not a good physical fit, that doesn't mean they won't be involved. They can always take other roles to help the team (e.g., observer, timer, planner).

Reduce, Reuse, Recycle

Activities-based training uses props over and over. Here is a list of all the props necessary to facilitate the activities in this book. For a green alternative to the problem-solving games (e.g., Car Pool), print out and laminate the clues and clue cards to use them over and over again.

Props

100-foot rope	Bandanas/blindfolds	Bouncy balls or tennis balls
3 × 5 cards	Paper	Spot markers or paper plates
Sticky notes	Hula hoops	Painter's or masking tape
Markers	Pens	Tarp or blanket
Clipboards	Stopwatch	Large Lego blocks

Have Fun out There

If you are looking for aha moments, nothing gets you there faster than team-building games. The team takes ownership by coming together to figure it out for themselves. They feel a sense of control and learn to trust each other as they stretch their collective comfort zones.

Best Program Ever!

Team-motivating games allow the team to create their own program: their own experience. Of course, that requires you, the trainer, to stretch your limits as well. Be ready to adapt: trust yourself and your team to rise to whatever challenge unfolds in the process. It's an exciting ride!

How to Use
This Book

Team-Motivating Games

These games are a special set of activities and exercises designed to improve communication, build trust, increase productivity, and generate camaraderie. Games can also provide experiences to support the objectives of a team meeting. As discussed in the introduction, team-motivating games have many benefits. Games are:

- Motivating
- Challenging
- Meaningful
- Easy to use
- Inexpensive
- Engaging
- Memorable
- Energizing
- Fun

In fact, many games provide a valuable lesson whether or not the participants succeed in a task. This is because the focus is on the process, the debrief discussion, and how the experience can be applied to the workplace. As an added bonus, games allow team members to have fun while learning.

Selecting an Appropriate Team-Motivating Game

As you look through this book, you'll notice that each team-building game has a distinct purpose, a recommended group size, a list of materials needed, and an estimated time requirement. Let these guidelines help you determine the appropriate games for your groups or meetings.

Preparing Game Materials

You will find it helpful to keep a supply of basic props that are often used in team-building games. Index cards, markers, masking tape, tennis balls, a deck of cards, rope, flip-chart paper, and even a ball of string are all quite useful. It is also worthwhile to look ahead and anticipate which games may be appropriate for a given group or meeting. After selecting one or more games, you can save time by preparing your handouts, flip charts, or presentations in advance.

Introducing a Game

In general, give a brief explanation and background for a game. It is important to provide a context for the activity to help the team see where it fits into the program's agenda. Get their attention, solicit their cooperation, and share appropriate information, such as any rules or guidelines. Then assign them their task, along with any time limits. Make sure to monitor the activity as it progresses, allowing ample time for the debrief discussion.

Leading a Team Discussion

Games will remain just that, games, in the absence of an effective facilitated debrief discussion. Look over the provided materials ahead of time. Anticipate probable results and reactions. Take notes throughout the activity. In addition to the debrief questions provided with the game's instructions, you may want to prepare other questions that are more tailored to suit your particular group or purpose. Indicate the time limits available for the debrief discussion. Focus the team's attention on the meaning and purpose behind the game. Encourage the participants to be responsible for generating meaningful conversation; don't be too quick to insert your own opinions and observations. Keep the discussion flowing, but also get comfortable with pauses as the group formulates their ideas and conclusions. End the discussion when all major points have been addressed.

Making the Transition to Applications

All of the games in this book are generic, meaning they are broad in nature and not restricted to any single organization or industry. Your debrief discussion, however, can be tailored to meet the specific needs of your group. As the facilitator, it is imperative that you shift the team's attention from what happened in the activity to what is significant about the results. Encourage participants to consider questions like, "What will we remember from the game tomorrow?" "What can we take from this experience?" and "How can we use this experience to improve our team's performance?" You may consider making a record of the key learning points raised and action plans developed to distribute to the team for later review and follow-up.

Tips for Using Team-Motivating Games

After more than two decades of experience with designing and conducting team-building games, we have learned a number of important lessons. Although these guidelines appear to be simple, they are vitally important to your success, as well as the success of your team.

1. **Have an objective.** Some facilitators and trainers jump into using a game without a well-thought-out, clear idea of what they hope to accomplish with the game. Simply put, they lack an objective, the logical starting point. As a result, a game may be chosen because it was

available, seemed handy, or looked interesting. You must do a thorough job of selecting games that fit your objectives—and then communicate that purpose to the team members.

2. **Select the specific game carefully.** Look through the entire set of games to develop familiarity with the nature of each game, the objectives, and the requirements (e.g., materials, time). Based on your objectives, choose one or more games to use with your group. Consider also whether the particular game is a good fit for your team's general nature and character, the objectives for the team's meeting, and the participants themselves.

3. **Pretest the game.** It's always a good idea to test-drive any of these games before using them with your participants. Close colleagues, volunteer staff, or family and friends can all be remarkably good critics. Seek them out and use them.

4. **Have a backup plan.** Especially when planning outdoor activities (where Mother Nature may choose not to cooperate), it is important to have more than one game prepared. Remember also that a prop might break, the participants may have played that particular game recently, or the team may be unresponsive to a certain type of game. It's good to be ready with an alternative.

In addition to these four general guidelines, here are some more tips for the use of games in team building.

- **Choose low-risk activities.** Keep in mind that your team's safety is your utmost concern. Be careful that you don't expose your team to unnecessary levels of physical or psychological risk. Screening the games beforehand will let you know if you can be comfortable leading the team through the experience.

- **Be brief and selective.** Time is a vital resource, and you and your participants can't afford to waste it. The majority of these games can be introduced and used in relatively short time periods. However, you are also provided with ample debrief questions if expanding the discussion proves to be desirable. Remember that the games themselves are not the focus of the team-building session. They are aids to achieve your goals and objectives. Don't drag the game out. Monitor the team's energy level and enthusiasm, and pace the activity accordingly.

- **Be creative.** Experiment a little. Search for ways to adapt or tailor a game to best fit your purpose for the team you're working with. Be on the lookout for new ways to make your point. Stay flexible.
- **Evaluate your use of games.** Keep close tabs on (1) the frequency with which you use games with a team, (2) the game's apparent impact on the team's learning and retention, and (3) the team's reaction to and reception of your games. It is easy to fall into ruts—we all have games we love to use—but take care not to overuse games to the detriment of the intended message. Challenge yourself to update and expand your repertoire of games for the good of your team.
- **Lighten up.** Take your task seriously, but don't take *yourself* too seriously. Team members will come to trust and believe in you when they see you as a real person—someone who can laugh at him- or herself and can be comfortable with minor deviations from the structured exercise. Above all, have fun and make it fun for the team.
- **Don't use games just to entertain.** High-performance teams want to be productive and use their time wisely; don't waste valuable meeting time by using a game solely to entertain or break up the workweek.
- **Be prepared.** After deciding to use a game, prepare for it thoroughly; never select one at the last minute. Make certain you are completely familiar with the game, your goals are clearly defined, and you have a specific plan for debriefing the team at the game's conclusion.
- **Know the answer (if one exists).** There is tremendous value in preparing a visual "key" that can be pulled out and displayed in case your mind goes blank while under pressure. Prepare a written "job aid" and keep it handy.
- **Anticipate some resistance.** You may occasionally encounter some team members who believe that games are "silly." If so, provide a clear explanation of the purpose of the activity, enlist the team's help in making it work, and promise them that the meaning will become clear during the debriefing.
- **Anticipate recall of the game, not the message.** Because games are different from a classic work-oriented agenda, there is always a

chance that team members will remember the game or activity and forget the underlying message. Once the game is completed and the meeting is nearly over, turn the group's attention once more to the key learning points.

Danger Zones in Using Games

We want you to succeed in your use of games for motivating your team. Therefore, we need to provide a balanced perspective on games by identifying some of the disadvantages and pitfalls to offset the enthusiasm exhibited throughout these introductory sections. Here are a series of potential difficulties or limitations, many of which can be minimized through careful planning and preparation.

1. **Props.** Some games require the use of props. Although these props are usually simple and conveniently available, some may prove to be inconvenient to obtain on short notice or to assemble in a hurry. Always leave yourself adequate lead time to gather materials before the session.
2. **Time.** Sometimes, games require more extended time than you are willing to devote. It is important to chart the process, monitor the discussion, and know when to bring the activity to an end.
3. **Preparation.** Games vary in the depth of background required to conduct them properly. Some require no special preparation, while others may be enriched by one's unique educational background or experience level. Group-processing skills—being able to draw people out in the debrief discussion—are essential to meeting your objectives as well.
4. **Perception.** Some participants may perceive certain games as being overly simplistic, while others will find them relevant and vivid. You need to gauge where your group is in relation to the game proposed, and perhaps pretest the game on one or two participants.

In addition to these structural limitations, there are other potential pitfalls in your use of games. It is possible that insecure, inexperienced, or unprepared individuals may use a game to kill time, to impress colleagues with how clever they are, or even to put some team members in their place by setting them up to fail. None of these actions are in the true spirit of team-building games. The games are designed to provide support for your key points, rather than to be the sole purpose of a meeting.

If your participants perceive that the games are "hokey" or cute, they may be distracted from the overall goal of the team meeting. You should always encourage team members to contribute answers to the questions of "So what?" "Now what?" or "What's in it for us?" for each game, and there should always be one or more substantive answers. Finally, good games should not become overly complicated, nor should they in any way be allowed to become personally threatening to any team member.

Summary

Games can contribute to both the content and process objectives of a team meeting. They facilitate learning and development of trust, while also making the meeting itself more enjoyable. Games can be used to:

- Break the ice
- Help create team identity
- Demonstrate the value of teamwork
- Encourage the appreciation of diversity
- Build mutual support and trust
- Improve the way the team functions
- Stimulate the realization that change is needed
- Uncover hidden problems
- Allow team members to feel a sense of community and connection
- Interject greater energy into team meetings
- Motivate the team to become better than they are now

Numerous guidelines have been presented to increase the likelihood of your success. These guidelines are directed toward the selection, use, and evaluation of games and are drawn from the experience of hundreds of applications. Above all, keep the games in their proper perspective; recognize that most are designed to help improve some facet of team performance, while injecting some fun in the process. Enjoy!

1

Icebreakers and Energizers

Whatever you can do, or dream you can, begin it. Boldness
has genius, power, and magic in it.

—Goethe

Answer the Question

OBJECTIVES
- To demonstrate the benefits of humor
- To increase the comfort level within the team

Group Size

10 to 20, or split large groups into smaller teams of 10 to 20

Materials

None

Time

10 to 20 minutes

Procedure

Have your team stand or sit in a circle. Tell them this activity consists of asking and answering questions. Let them know they will ask the person next to them an open-ended question (one requiring more than a yes-or-no answer). Specifically, questions that require the person to answer with a sentence, rather than simply one word, work best. Instruct each participant to remember the question he or she asked, as well as the answer given.

To start the game, simply have one team member ask the person on his or her right or left a question. This establishes the direction: for example, if the team member asks the person to the right, that person answers and then asks a question to the person to his or her right, and so on around the circle. By the time you get around the circle, everyone should have asked and answered a question. Remind the team members to remember their question and their answer.

Now for the fun part: have everyone get up and take a different place in the circle so they are standing or sitting next to someone new. To start this round, again have one team member ask the person to the right or left his or her *original* question (again establishing the direction), and have everyone give his or her *original* answer—regardless of the question.

Get ready to laugh!

Discussion Questions

1. What did you like about this activity? What was challenging?
2. How does laughter impact our energy? Our productivity? Our teamwork? Our stress level?
3. What are some other ways to reduce the stress level within our teams?

Fun Facts

A Triplet

Loves to Run

Went to ASU

Procedure

Some prep work is required. Have all the team members who will attend submit a few little-known facts about themselves to you—the facilitator—before the session (e.g., where they went to school, their major, number of siblings, names of pets, where they were born, favorite vacation spot).

Before the meeting, write a statement about each person based on the submitted facts. Put all the statements together on the Fun Facts About Our Team form, and give everyone a copy as they come in.

Give the team time to mingle and ask each other questions to determine whose name belongs with each statement. Let them know they also need to find out any specifics. For example, if they have three pets, what kind of animals are they? What are their names?

Whoever has the most names filled in after about 10 minutes gets to announce the team members along with their little-known facts.

Example Statement Sheet (or use the provided Fun Facts About Our Team form)

Born in a country other than the United States

- Name of the person _____
- Name of the country _____

Changed my major in college three times

- Name of the person _____
- The three different majors _____

Fun Facts About Our Team

Fact _____

- Name of the person _____

- Details _____

Fact _____

- Name of the person _____

- Details _____

Fact _____

- Name of the person _____

- Details _____

Fact _____

- Name of the person _____

- Details _____

Fact _____

- Name of the person _____

- Details _____

Fact _____

- Name of the person _____

- Details _____

Guess Me If You Can

OBJECTIVES
- To get to know each other
- To come together as a team

Group Size

10 to 20 participants works best

Materials

Slips of paper, pens

Time

15 to 20 minutes per round

Procedure

Have each participant write out the name of a book (or movie, etc.—see other categories under Variations) on a slip of paper. One person acts as the facilitator and collects and reads aloud all the slips of paper *one time.* After that, everyone must rely on their memory.

The person to the left of the facilitator begins by trying to match a book title with the person who chose it. If the guesser is correct, the person whose book was guessed becomes a member of the guesser's team, and as a team they take another turn. Every correct guess gains the team an additional team member and gives them another turn. If they're wrong, the next person takes a turn, and so on around the team.

The activity is over when everyone is on the same team.

Variations

Instead of book titles, you can use movie titles, song titles, musical groups, board games, cities, vacation spots, and so on. Get creative! Or have the team come up with some new categories. Remember, the goal is to make it challenging for the others to guess the selections.

Discussion Questions

1. What did you notice as we made the transition from individuals to teams, and finally to one team?

2. What does it take to be a team?

3. In what ways does this relate to coming together as a team at work?

Partner Stretch

Group Size

Any

Materials

None

Time

5 minutes to develop stretches, and 1 minute
per pair to teach and lead a three-count

Procedure

Have the team pair up. Then have each pair
develop a quick stretch that they will teach the
rest of the team.

The stretch has two requirements: (1) the partners have to be connected
during the stretch, and (2) the stretch has to have a sound effect or phrase
to go along with it. Each pair then teaches their stretch to the team and
takes the team through a three-count of the stretch.

Demonstrate an example of an acceptable stretch. For example, stand
next to your partner, with your and your partner's feet touching; then
stretch your arms up and say, "Reach for the stars."

Variations

For larger groups or if time is tight, after each pair has developed their
stretch, have them group together with two other pairs and teach each
other their stretches.

Discussion Questions

1. What did you notice regarding your energy level as well as the overall energy level in the room during this activity?

2. What are some things we can do to raise our energy when it's low, such as after lunch or at the end of the day?

Tips

This activity works great as a midafternoon energizer.

Shout Out

Group Size

10 to 20 participants

Materials

Large blanket or tarp

Time

10 minutes

Procedure

Ask for two volunteers to hold the blanket up, creating a wall. Split the rest of the team in half. Have half the team go on one side of the blanket and half go on the other.

Each team sends a person up to the blanket—taking care that the people on the other side of the blanket can't see who is chosen.

The volunteers count, "1, 2, 3, drop!" Then they quickly lower the blanket to the ground. The person who says the other person's name first acquires that person to his or her side of the blanket. (The volunteer blanket holders act as judges, and their decisions may break any ties that occur.)

Continue for about five to eight minutes. Lift the blanket at the end and say, "Now we are all one team again."

Discussion Questions

1. Was that activity more challenging that you expected it to be? Why?

2. Why did we make mistakes?

3. How did the team react to mistakes?

4. What is an effective way to handle mistakes at work?

Table Topics

OBJECTIVES

- To establish rapport before brainstorming and problem-solving activities
- To increase the level of trust within the team

Group Size

Up to 15, or break large groups into smaller teams of 5 to 7

Materials

Copies of the Table Topics form (provided)

Time

10 to 15 minutes

Procedure

This one is easy. Make copies of the Table Topics form or create some of your own.

At the beginning of the workshop or whenever participants regroup into smaller work teams, have each team go around their table and answer three to five questions.

Tips

After answering a couple of prepared questions, they can come up with a couple of their own to ask.

Table Topics

1. If you could pick a theme song that would play whenever you entered a room, what would it be?

2. What do you most admire about the person to your left?

3. What do you consider to be the best thing ever invented? Why?

4. If you could move anywhere for one year, where would it be?

5. What is your most compulsive daily ritual?

6. What is the oddest job you have ever had?

7. What is your favorite way to spend a relaxing weekend day?

8. What are your pet peeves in the workplace?

9. In what way are you superstitious?

10. What have you not done that you have wanted to do for years?

11. What's your dream job?

12. What are the most important qualities you look for in a friend?

13. What one goal would you like to accomplish this year?

14. What part of your personality would you most like to change?

15. What is one fear you'd like to overcome?

16. What is your favorite quotation?

17. What is the most beautiful place you have ever seen?

18. What negative experience have you had that turned out to be for the best?

2

Climate Setting

Teamwork is the ability to work together toward a common vision. The ability to direct individual accomplishments toward organizational objectives. It is the fuel that allows common people to attain uncommon results.

—Andrew Carnegie

Act the Part

OBJECTIVES

- To consider what it takes to be understood
- To encourage effective communication strategies

Group Size

At least 10 participants

Materials

Slips of paper, pens

Time

20 minutes

Procedure

Each team will partner with another team, so split the group into teams of five to seven (this game works best if all teams have the same number of participants). Pass out slips of paper and pens to each team. Ask each team to come up with an animal and a common task. Have them write it on their slip of paper as a sentence (e.g., "An elephant rides a bike," or "A monkey brushes his teeth.").

Have two teams line up facing the same direction. The two teams will work in conjunction. Have the last persons in each line exchange slips of paper. After this point, the rest of the activity is carried out nonverbally. The last person in each line is the only person allowed to see the slip of paper. His or her job is to convey this message to the person ahead in line by acting it out.

So the person ahead of the last person turns and looks on while the last person acts out the scenario written on the slip of paper. The second to the last person then acts it out for the person ahead in line. This continues up to the first person in line. The first person in each line acts out the scenario so participants from both small teams can see.

Have each team guess what it is they have been acting out. How close do they come to the original scenario?

Tips

This is a good climate-setting activity. You may consider skipping the discussion, and just go right into the next thing on your agenda. In case you do choose to discuss, some questions follow.

Discussion Questions

1. How effective was your communication?

2. What helped you communicate effectively?

3. Was it easier to communicate nonverbally than you thought it would be?

4. How powerful is nonverbal communication?

5. How effective is nonverbal communication?

Inside Out

Group Size

Any

Materials

Inside Out suggested topic questions (provided)

Time

10 to 15 minutes

Procedure

Have the team form two circles, one inside the other. The inside circle faces out; the outside circle faces in. Position the circles so each person is standing face to face with someone in the other circle. If you have an odd number of participants, there will be one triad.

Inform the team that they will be on the move during this activity, as you're going to keep them on their feet. Let them know you will give them a topic for discussion. They will have one minute to discuss the topic with their partner before it is time to move on.

Give them the first topic to discuss. When the minute is up, yell out, "Time to move on," and instruct them how to move. Choose how they will move: for example, the outside circle moves two people to the left, or inside circles move one person to the right. The idea is that every time the team members move, they get new and different partners. Once everyone has a new partner, the next round of conversations starts with a new topic.

After each round and before moving on, make sure each person gives his or her partner some form of "thank you"—a pat on the back, a high five, a verbal "Thanks for chatting," or some form of appreciation. Get creative!

Tips

It's best to keep this one moving rather than let the conversation die down before continuing to the next partner and next topic.

Playing four or five rounds seems to work best. After the final topic has been discussed, you may choose to give them one more minute to share their goals for the day with this final partner.

The questions for Table Topics will work for this activity as well.

Discussion Questions

1. How did it feel to divulge personal information?

2. How does an activity like this build trust within the team?

3. What are some other ways we can build a trusting team?

Inside Out

Suggested Topic Questions

1. If money wasn't an issue, what career would you choose? Why?

2. What is the easiest way to annoy you or push your buttons?

3. What person in your life has had the greatest impact on you? In what way?

4. What have you done in the past year that has been completely out of character for you?

5. Tell a story about yourself that would surprise everyone.

6. If talent weren't an issue, what career would you choose for yourself?

7. What is your one guilty pleasure?

8. What do you wish you had time to do every day? How could you make that time?

9. What is your favorite vacation spot? Why?

May I Present . . . ?

OBJECTIVES
- To allow team members to gain a better understanding of each other
- To encourage participants to share information in a fun way
- To introduce each other to the team

Group Size

20 participants works best

Materials

Flip chart or whiteboard, blank sheets of paper, markers, adhesive tape

Time

30 to 45 minutes

Procedure

Have participants pair up. Provide each pair with blank sheets of paper and markers. Write these instructions on a flip chart or whiteboard so everyone can see them:

On the first sheet of paper, write your partner's name and draw a picture of your partner. On the second sheet of paper, create a fact sheet by writing down your partner's answers to the following questions:

- *What do you like about your job?*
- *What are the skills you admire in others?*
- *What would we be surprised to know about you?*

Have each team member introduce his or her partner by presenting the drawing and the answers to the three questions. After the presentations, tape all the drawings and fact sheets to the walls for the duration of the program.

Red Card/Green Card

Group Size

Any

Materials

Red and green 3 × 5 cards

Time

10 minutes

Procedure

Pass out one red or green 3 × 5 card to each team member (half the team getting one color, half getting the other color). Explain that the color of the card they are holding indicates the type of first impression they will be creating during the activity.

Those with green cards like meeting others and enjoy interacting. Ask the team what they would do to create that type of face-to-face impression (e.g., make eye contact, smile, shake hands).

People with red cards, on the other hand, don't care about interpersonal relationships. In fact, life would be just great if all those other people weren't out there. They would be content to go crawl in a corner and be left alone! Have the team describe what they would do to create that type of first impression (e.g., avoid eye contact, give short answers, use negative body language).

Now tell the team that on your "Go," they will have a chance to create a first impression with everyone else in the room. That impression should be based on the color of the card they received. Have them interact with as many people as possible in 25 seconds. (They don't have to carry their cards during the activity. In fact, it's best if they don't—that will better demonstrate the power of first impressions.)

Discussion Questions

1. Green Cards, could you tell who the Red Cards were? How could you tell?
2. Red Cards, when the Green Cards approached you, was it difficult to maintain your Red Card demeanor? Why?
3. Why is it important to create a positive first impression?

Shake It Up

Group Size

Any

Materials

None

Time

15 to 20 minutes

Procedure

Have participants pair up. Each pair is required to come up with a hand-shake. The handshake has to have three moves and a sound effect or phrase. Give them a few minutes to develop and practice their handshake.

Have each pair team up with another pair. Have them put their hand-shakes together to form a six-part handshake with two sound effects. Give the new foursomes time to practice.

Have each foursome join with another foursome to put their handshakes together for a twelve-part, four-sound-effect handshake. Time permitting, have each team of eight present their handshakes to the whole group.

Variations

You can stop this at four or continue with the eight-person version (more challenging). There are many ways to adapt this one, depending on the number of people you have in your team.

Discussion Questions

1. How did you learn the twelve-part handshake without becoming overwhelmed?

2. What aspect about this process was easy? Challenging?

3. In what ways does this relate to sharing information and learning from each other at work?

Knick Knack

Group Size

8 to 12 works best

Materials

Koosh ball and hacky sack (or any two different, small props)

Time

10 minutes

Procedure

Circle up the team. In your right hand hold a koosh ball or something similar. In your left hand hold a hacky sack or similar (any two different types of items will work).

Show the koosh ball to the person on your right, and say, "This is a knick." To which the person on your right responds, "A what?" You reply, "A knick." The person responds by saying, "Thank you," and takes the knick.

He then repeats the process with the person on his right, except when she says, "A what?" instead of responding, he turns back to you and repeats, "A what?" to you.

You reply, "A knick," which he then repeats to the person who just asked him. After answering with a thank you, she takes the knick, then shows it to the next person and says, "This is a knick."

That person responds with, "A what?" and the "A whats" continue back to you. You again respond, "A knick," which is passed person to person back to the person who is about to be presented with the knick.

With each repetition of passing of the knick, heads turn back and forth as the questions and answers make the way around the circle.

While all this is taking place with the knick, the same process is transpiring in the opposite direction with the knack.

Discussion

1. What was your biggest challenge in this activity?

2. Why was it so difficult to keep track of what you were doing?

3. What are some of the downfalls of hopping back and forth between tasks, rather than focusing on one thing?

4. What are some ways multitasking impacts the team?

3

Motivation

Ability is what you're capable of doing. Motivation determines what you do. Attitude determines how well you do it.

—Lou Holtz

The Bucket List

OBJECTIVES

• To create a personal vision board consisting of goals and visions

Group Size

Any

Materials

Various magazines (a large variety to provide inspiration), scissors, glue stick or adhesive tape, poster board or flip-chart paper, markers

Time

20 to 30 minutes

Procedure

Distribute one sheet of poster board or flip chart paper to each person to create his or her vision board. Ask everyone to consider what their goals are for the next three to five years. With their goals in mind, invite everyone to cut out any words or pictures from the magazines that resonate with those goals and dreams to create their personalized vision board. Next, have the team members write out their own personal vision statement, mission statement, and goals for the next three to five years based on their vision boards.

While this is largely an individual activity, working with a team and being able to share ideas helps clarify ideas and provide insight for the individuals. Since the vision boards, vision statements, and mission statements can be a source of inspiration for the team members, have them present to the group or post them in appropriate locations in their work areas. If you use a high-quality heavy-weight paper, the overall look and feel of the finished product will be a high-quality reminder of the goals they set that day.

Variations

You can easily adapt this activity to reflect the team's vision and mission. Then it's essential to create a high-quality product that can be posted for the team to see on a regular basis.

Tips

Encourage accountability by scheduling a follow-up. Have each person exchange contact information with at least one other person and commit to getting in touch with that person in two weeks to follow up with each other's progress. Have them put it on their schedules right away.

Notes

Quick definitions, in case your team needs further explanation:

- **Vision:** what you want to be when you grow up; how you see the future
- **Mission:** telling the world who you are, what you do, and how you do it in 25 words or less
- **Goals:** general statements of your direction for the next few years
- **Objectives:** specific tasks and tactics to accomplish your goals; typically, objectives follow a SMART (i.e., specific, measurable, attainable, realistic, time-bound) concept

Discussion Questions

1. Even though our goals and vision or mission statements are highly personal, what impact could it have to open up and share this information as we are doing today?
2. Now that you have created this vision for yourself, what is the next step?
3. How can you implement that step and future steps?

How Do We Stack Up?

OBJECTIVES
- To show how we create the context of our work
- To generate ideas for improving motivation in the workplace

Group Size

Any

Materials

12 plastic cups for each team, stopwatch

Time

20 to 30 minutes

Procedure

Split large groups into teams of seven. Each team gets 12 plastic cups. Next, demonstrate how to stack and unstack the cups by making three pyramids of cups. The pyramids on the left and right have two cups as a base and one on top. The stack in the middle is a three-two-one-cup pyramid: three on the bottom, two in the middle, and one on top. Each team has six stackers and one timer. If you have extra team members, you can improvise the requirements or assign an "observer" or two. The teams time themselves doing the task and then have two additional attempts to improve their time.

The task: the first person stacks, the second unstacks, the third stacks, the fourth unstacks, the fifth stacks, and the sixth unstacks. To begin, the first person places his or her hands on the table and on "Go" starts stacking. The clock stops when the sixth person places his or her hands on the table. Unstacking can begin only after the stacker has completed all three stacks.

Discussion Questions

1. What did your team do to improve productivity?

2. What was the "task"? What was the "context" your team created?

3. How could we create a similar context with our tasks at work?

Tips

This activity is a great springboard for a discussion of task and context. Any task is neutral—neither good nor bad, neither fun nor boring. The context we create makes the task rewarding.

The Office

OBJECTIVES
- To assess our attitudes and how they impact our energy and motivation
- To demonstrate that focusing on the negative aspects of a situation depletes energy levels, while focusing on the positive aspects increases energy levels

Group Size

Up to 20

Materials

Flip charts, markers, space enough for two discussion groups

Time

30 minutes

Procedure

Split the group in half. Each group gets a flip chart and markers.

The first group discusses a bad work experience (e.g., poor leadership, bad environment, difficult coworker) from a *previous* job. Have them record their ideas along with illustrations on the flip chart.

The second group discusses a positive work experience (e.g., great boss, great company philosophy, good camaraderie, supportive coworkers) past *or* present. Have them record their discussion along with illustrations on their flip chart.

While the groups are talking, provide any necessary coaching. Also, notice the differences in the overall energy and enthusiasm, or better yet, ask a couple of participants to act as observers—they can provide valuable insight in the debrief discussion. Have them take notes about what they observe.

After 10 to 15 minutes, bring everyone together. Have each group give a brief presentation of their highlights of bad and good experiences. The group who discussed bad experiences goes first. When the group who discussed their positive experiences is finished, jump right into the debrief discussion.

Tips

After the presentations, you may want to let the team who discussed bad work experiences know that you appreciate the residual emotions they experienced due to their discussion and thank them for their willingness to endure those emotions one more time.

After the debrief discussion, do a fun energizing game such as Partner Stretch to raise the overall energy level.

Discussion Questions

1. How did you feel when discussing your poor experiences?

2. Observers: What did you notice?

3. When we focus on the negative, energy levels tend to go down and as a result we feel drained. By focusing on the positive, our energy levels go up and we feel energized. If energy is motivation, how can we use this information to improve our current work team and environment?

Picture This

OBJECTIVES
- To keep track of information gained in the program
- To create a takeaway from the program

Group Size

Any

Materials

Copies of the What I Got from This Training form (provided)

Time

15 minutes

Procedure

At the end of a workshop, pass out a copy of the What I Got from This Training form to every team member. Ask participants to fill in each box with tips, information, and takeaways regarding their experience.

After five minutes, have them work in small teams of four or five to share ideas and add to their forms.

Open the discussion to the entire team, inviting participants to continue to add to their forms as necessary.

Variations

Pass out the form at the *beginning* of a workshop, and encourage participants to add to the form as they wish throughout the day, or provide time before breaks to track their thoughts and share ideas. As a review, go over the discussion questions at the end of the program.

Discussion Questions

1. How do you feel about your experience today? To what do you attribute those feelings?

2. What knowledge or information will you take from today? Where did that knowledge come from? How can you continue to learn from each other after this workshop?

3. What new ideas did you come away with? What were some good reminders?

4. What action do you plan to take as a result of your experience today?

What I Got from This Training

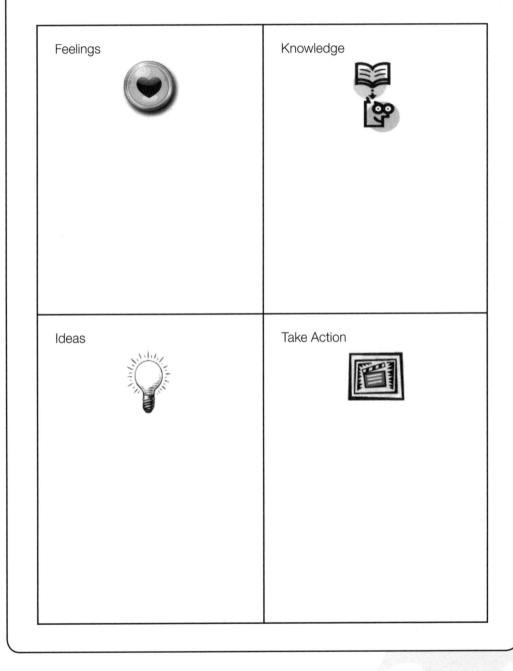

Feelings	Knowledge

Ideas	Take Action

The Whole Picture

Group Size

Any

Materials

Flip-chart paper or poster board for each group, markers

Time

20 to 30 minutes

Procedure

Have participants form groups of four to seven. Provide each group with flip-chart paper and markers.

The groups must create a drawing that depicts the qualities of a successful team, including the individual contributions that are necessary to bring out those qualities. For example, the group could draw a sun. In the middle of the sun, they could write all the qualities that make up a team (trust, communication, etc.). On the rays coming out of the sun, they could write team members' contributions (e.g., be a good listener, help each other, be reliable).

After 15 minutes, have the groups present their posters to the whole team.

Tips

Rather than stifle any creativity, let the groups run with this one. Prepare to be amazed!

Discussion Questions

1. What are some ways these qualities and characteristics were demonstrated throughout this program?

2. What can we do to ensure we incorporate these qualities and characteristics into our everyday work?

We're Number 1!

OBJECTIVES
- To create a strong team identity
- To make tangible the concept of "team"

Group Size

Up to 28

Materials

Flip-chart paper; markers; construction paper; adhesive tape; scissors; assorted craft materials such as foam, pipe cleaners, feathers, felt squares, and stickers

Time

20 to 30 minutes

Procedure

In this game, the team has the job of creating their own unique identity. Just as their favorite sports teams have logos and mascots, so will the team.

The first step is to brainstorm, so divide any large team into groups of four to seven people. Ask them to think about the team they have come together to create. (Remember this is the *whole* team they are considering, not just the four to seven members of each brainstorming group.) Ask each group to take four minutes to brainstorm about who they are and what they are all about.

To start the discussion, write out these questions on a flip chart or whiteboard:

- How would you describe our team?
- What do we do well?
- Who are we as individuals?
- What are we like?
- What's great about our team?

After their brainstorming sessions, bring the whole team together to discuss their ideas about who they are and what they are all about. These ideas can be tracked on a flip chart by the facilitator or a volunteer from the team. Now that everyone "is on the same page," you can divide up the work. Assign each group a different task:

1. Figure out a team name.
2. Come up with a team logo.
3. Create a team mascot.
4. Write a team slogan.

When all of the groups are finished, have them present their portion of the new team identity.

Variations

Have each group develop all four components of the team ID. When all of the groups are finished, have them pitch their team ID to the whole group. The whole group then decides which team ID best describes them or takes components from different groups to create their team ID.

Discussion Questions

1. In what ways does it benefit the team to have an identity?
2. What are some creative ways we can incorporate our identity into our daily work environment?

Worst Team Ever

OBJECTIVES
- To raise awareness of the obstacles to creating a great team
- To become the best team ever!

Group Size
Any

Materials
Flip-chart paper, markers

Time
20 to 30 minutes

Procedure

Split the team members into groups of five to seven. Give each group flip-chart paper and markers. The groups then have 20 minutes to create a poster depicting the worst team ever, including the qualities and characteristics of the worst team and an illustration. After 20 minutes, have the groups present their work.

Tips

You may have to monitor this so it does not turn into a gripe session. It is meant to be done in fun and have a positive outcome.

Discussion Questions

1. Have we all experienced or displayed some of these qualities? Why? What can we do about it?
2. In your discussion of the worst team ever, did you come up with some qualities of the best team ever? What were those?
3. How can this activity help us become the best team ever?
4. What is our individual responsibility in creating the best team ever?

The Rain in Spain

Group Size
Any

Materials
Flip-chart paper, marker

Time
10 to 15 minutes

Procedure

Prepare a flip-chart page by writing down a definition of the Pygmalion effect:

> *The Pygmalion effect: Once an expectation is set, even if inaccurate, we tend to behave in ways that are consistent with that expectation. Surprisingly often, the result is the expectation, as if by magic, comes true.*

Ask the group if they are familiar with the musical *My Fair Lady*. Review for them the premise that people often rise to the level of expectations that others or they themselves set. In fact, a number of studies have verified that this approach to working with people really works.

In groups of three or four, ask teams to discuss examples they have heard about or perhaps were even involved in personally wherein a manager or team leader used this principle.

Discussion Questions

1. What have you heard about the Pygmalion effect?

2. Can you think of any examples when a superior, manager, or perhaps a teacher may have employed this idea?

3. Have you ever used this principle with any of your own team members? How about with your boss? Anyone in your own family? What was the result?

4. Can you see any downside to following this principle?

4

Communication

It is a luxury to be understood.

—Ralph Waldo Emerson

Attitude Adjustment

OBJECTIVES
- To discover the power of attitude
- To realize we control our attitude, which impacts our energy and motivation

Group Size
Any

Materials
None

Time
10 to 15 minutes

Procedure

Have the team members pair up. This activity consists of two rounds. Each person will have a chance to relay some information. Have the partners decide who will go first (or just assign the person with the shortest commute, biggest shoes, or some other fun characteristic).

Round One: The first person tells his partner something he enjoys doing or something he has a passion for. Give him one minute, and then it's the other person's turn. Discuss how they communicated their passions.

Round Two: The first person tells *the same story* he did before, except now he is having a very bad day, woke up on the wrong side of the bed, and just doesn't care. The difference is the attitude. Give each partner one minute to share this version of the story. Discuss how they communicated their negative attitudes.

Tips

Be ready with a quick energizer to end on a high note! For an easy one, just have participants put their pens between their teeth, forcing their faces into a smiling position. This has been proven to send out energy-enhancing endorphins. Ta-da!

Discussion Questions

1. What did you notice about the energy level during the two rounds of play?

2. If we can turn these positives into negatives so easily, is it possible to turn negatives into positives just as easily? Why or why not?

3. What is the benefit of adjusting our attitude? How does this impact the team?

4. What are some strategies we could use to do this?

Draw

OBJECTIVES

- To allow team members to consider the drawbacks of one-way communication
- To encourage participants to clarify their understanding when receiving messages

Group Size

This activity works best for up to 12 participants. For a large group, split into smaller teams.

Materials

Copies of the drawing handout (provided), additional sheets of paper, pens

Time

10 to 20 minutes

Procedure

Have all the participants stand one behind the other in a single line. Briefly show the original drawing to the last person in line. With her finger, she "draws" the picture on the back of the person in front of her, who then draws on the back of the person in front of him or her, and so on down the line to the first person. When the first person in the line finally gets the "message," he or she draws it on a sheet of paper.

Compare all the final drawings with the original to see how many different messages were received.

Discussion Questions

1. When does communication start to break down?
2. What are some reasons for our communication breakdown?
3. What can we do to make sure our message is understood?
4. What did you learn about communication that you can take back to the workplace?

Draw Picture

Human Emoticons

OBJECTIVES

- To demonstrate the power of body language in our face-to-face communication
- To increase our awareness of the messages we send nonverbally

Group Size

Any

Materials

Copies of the Human Emoticon Cards cut-outs and the Human Emoticons handout (all provided), additional sheets of paper, pens

Time

10 to 20 minutes

Procedure

Prior to the session, cut out the Human Emoticon Cards, or copy the words onto 3 × 5 cards (be sure to number the cards).

Ask for volunteers to play a quick game of emoticons—a game where they will demonstrate an emotion without using any words or sounds. Because there are 12 Human Emoticon cards, 12 volunteers would be ideal. Allow each volunteer to choose a card; then ask all the volunteers to leave the room to prepare for their roles. Give them two to three minutes to practice their roles and help the other volunteers.

Tell those who are still in the room that they are not to shout out their response to each demonstration. Rather they can write down their interpretation on their copy of the Human Emoticons handout or a numbered sheet of paper. (This will open up a discussion on interpretation.)

Call the volunteers in, and one at a time, have each one act out the emotion on his or her Human Emoticon Card. Have the rest of the team write down their interpretations of all the emoticons being demonstrated. After the 12 demonstrations, check to see if the respondents gave the "correct" interpretation.

Variations

For an alternative that uses less paper, you could have participants shout out their guesses. Have the volunteers make a note of the guesses on the back of their cards. Then discuss the guesses after all the volunteers have presented their roles.

Discussion Questions

1. How powerful is nonverbal communication?
2. Do we all interpret nonverbal messages in the same way? Why not? What is the "correct" interpretation?
3. Based on this activity, what are some things we should keep in mind regarding the messages we send nonverbally?

Human Emoticon Cards

Copy and cut out the following cards to hand out to your team.

1. Sadness	2. Amusement
3. Shock	4. Curiosity
5. Anger	6. Surprise
7. Disbelief	8. Understanding
9. Happiness	10. Fear
11. Excitement	12. Confusion

Human Emoticons

My Interpretation	*Their Intention*
1. _____	1. _____
2. _____	2. _____
3. _____	3. _____
4. _____	4. _____
5. _____	5. _____
6. _____	6. _____
7. _____	7. _____
8. _____	8. _____
9. _____	9. _____
10. _____	10. _____
11. _____	11. _____
12. _____	12. _____

Oh

Group Size

Any

Materials

Sheet of paper and pen

Time

10 to 20 minutes

Procedure

This is a fast and fun way to demonstrate the power of tone in our verbal communication.

As the facilitator, write the word "Oh" on a sheet of paper so everyone on the team can see it. Ask them to say the word, and lead them in saying the word aloud. Now tell them the following:

The simple word "Oh" says very little as you see it written here. However, when we say the word "Oh," it can have many different meanings according to how it is spoken. I am going to read you some different intentions, and after I read each one, please convey that intention by saying the word "Oh" in the appropriate tone of voice.

Then read each of the following intentions, and wait for the team to verbally demonstrate the tone. You may want to say it with them for the first one to get them started.

- You surprised me!
- I made a mistake.
- You're a pain in the neck.

- You make me so happy.
- I'm bored.
- I'm fascinated.
- I understand.
- I don't understand.

Variations

Use the word "Dude," or run through the list twice using both words.

Discussion Questions

1. How can one word mean so many different things?

2. What can this simple activity teach us about the power of tone?

3. What is a good takeaway from this activity?

Orange Siblings

Group Size

Any

Materials

Copies of the Script: The Orange Siblings cutout (provided); for a neat visual, you can have an orange, a paper plate, and a plastic knife for each pair

Time

15 minutes

Procedure

Have the participants pair up. Pass out copies of the script cutout: one partner gets the Valencia cutout; the other gets the Navel cutout. Each person reads his or her cutout and can share only the information that is specifically requested by his or her partner. Give them a minute to read their script; then have them start their negotiations.

Discussion Questions

1. Did anyone have to cut their orange in half? Why was that necessary—or not?
2. What was your outcome? How did you reach it?
3. Was there a potential for win-win in this negotiation?
4. Do we look for a win-win in our negotiations? What does it take to get there?

Script: The Orange Siblings

Navel Orange

Navel and Valencia, the Orange siblings, are persistent, goal oriented, and willing to do what it takes to get their needs met. They are determined, are a bit stubborn, and can be competitive.

Navel, you are an aspiring chef. In fact, one of your newest culinary creations has been entered in a major competition. The prize is a one-week internship with your favorite chef, Emeril Lagasse.

Your scone recipe calls for orange zest, which you get by grating the rind of the orange. You have a tight deadline, so you don't have time to run to the store. Not to worry, there is one orange left at home. But wait . . . your sibling is reaching for it . . . you had better start negotiating!

Valencia Orange

Navel and Valencia, the Orange siblings, are persistent, goal oriented, and willing to do what it takes to get their needs met. They are determined, are a bit stubborn, and can be competitive.

Valencia, you are the health nut of the family. You are dedicated to healthy living; therefore, you are very disciplined and strict with whatever plan you're on.

Your newest fitness regimen calls for freshly squeezed orange juice at precisely 4 P.M., which is fast approaching. Not to worry, there is one orange left at home. But wait . . . your sibling is reaching for it . . . you had better start negotiating!

Say What?

Group Size

Any

Materials

None

Time

10 to 15 minutes

Procedure

This quick activity demonstrates what it takes to be understood. Divide the group into three teams, and line them up in three parallel lines (large groups can be divided into smaller three-team groups). The object of the game is for the team on one side to try to get a message to the team on the other side, while the team in the middle tries to drown out the message in any way they can.

- Team 1 is the message sender.
- Team 2 is the message receiver.
- Team 3 provides distraction.

Give teams a few minutes to strategize before beginning. The message-sending team will also need time to come up with a message to send (at least three sentences in length).

Play enough rounds so that each team can play each role.

Discussion Questions

1. How did you get your message across?

2. What did the message senders do to ensure you *received* the correct message?

3. Did your strategy change during the activity? In what way?

4. How many different ways were used to communicate messages?

5. Which ways were most effective? Why?

6. What are some reasons our messages get "drowned out" in the workplace? What can we do to prevent that from happening?

What's Your Story?

Group Size

Any

Materials

None

Time

10 minutes

Procedure

Have everyone find a partner. Tell each pair to decide which of them will be the first storyteller. The storyteller has two minutes to tell the partner a story. Story topics could include a recent vacation, a funny situation, an interesting experience, or a hobby. The listening partner's job is simply to listen. After two minutes, have them switch roles.

The next step is for everyone to find new partners. This time, the story they just heard has now become "their story." They have two minutes each to convey that story to their new partner as if it happened to them.

Discussion Questions

1. How well did you listen?
2. If the original person had been sitting next to you, how well would that person think you captured his or her story?
3. What does it take to be an effective listener?

Stuck like Glue

Group Size

   10 to 30

Materials

   Painter's tape or rope

Time

   15 to 20 minutes

Procedure

Create a start line and finish line four or five feet apart. The line needs to be long enough so the team members can stand side by side during the activity. Have the team stand behind the start line, and let them know that their goal is to reach the finish line as a team. To ensure they work as a team, each team member must have his or her feet "glued" to the person next to him or her (the outsides of the feet must remain in constant contact). While crossing from the start to the finish line, if anyone on the team's feet become unconnected, the whole team starts over.

Tips

The larger the group, the shorter the expanse from the start line to the finish line. For 10 participants, five or six feet is fine. If you have between 20 and 30 on your team, keep the distance between three and four feet. It can be challenging for 30 people to coordinate their moves to reach their goal.

Discussion Questions

1. How was the communication within the team?

2. Were all ideas heard? Why or why not?

3. How did the team come together to achieve success?

4. What did you learn?

5

Building Trust

You can't shake hands with a clenched fist.

—Mahatma Gandhi

Back to Back

Group Size

Any

Materials

Paper, pens, Sample Drawing Templates (provided), clipboard (optional)

Time

15 minutes

Procedure

Have the participants pair up and sit back to back. One person—the *artist*—gets the clipboard and pen; the other—the *director*—gets a template of a picture. The director's goal is to get the artist to draw an exact duplicate of the picture by using only verbal directions. (Sample templates are provided with this game.)

The first time through the exercise, the director describes to the artist what to draw, but the artist is not allowed to speak to the director. For the second round, have the partners switch roles, and hand out the second template. This time, for the first five minutes only allow the artist to ask yes-or-no questions. After the five minutes are up, allow the artist to ask any questions he or she would like.

When the partners are done with both rounds, they can compare drawings.

Discussion Questions

1. What was it like to give directions without getting any feedback?

2. Once you could ask questions, did that make the job easier? Why?

3. What kind of questions were the most effective?

4. What types of situations resemble this activity?

5. What can we do to improve our communication with each other?

Sample Drawing Template 1

Sample Drawing Template 2

Flying Blind

Group Size

6 to 12 participants works best

Materials

20-foot rope or painter's tape; a blindfold; facilitator-prepared written instructions; props required by the written instructions, such as a chair, cup, water bottle, hat, and sunglasses

Time

15 to 20 minutes

Procedure

Create a 20-foot starting line with rope or tape. The facilitator will need to prepare written instructions based on the props the team will use in this challenge.

Ask the group to select their best listener. Bring that person 20 feet in front of the starting line and blindfold the person. At this point, the listener cannot speak until the game is over and cannot move unless told to do so.

Ask the group to select their best communicator. Bring that person forward 10 feet and turn the person to face the group, who should all be standing on the starting line. The communicator may not turn around to look behind, but he or she is allowed to speak. The group on the starting line cannot say anything until the game is over.

Now produce some props: a chair, a hoop, a hat, a glass, a bottle of water, and so on. Give the set of written instructions to the group on the starting line, for example:

Have the communicator direct the listener to put on the hat, sit on the chair, pour him- or herself a cup of water, and then drink it!

Without speaking, the group has to make the communicator understand the directions so he or she can tell the listener what to do.

Notes

"Mouthing" and whispering the directions to the communicator are not permitted. Only miming is allowed!

Tips

If you have a large group and lots of space, run two or three games simultaneously (as long as the communicators can't see the props). The facilitator will then prepare different written instructions for each team. If you have a few more than the optimal number, you could assign some team members to be observers.

Discussion Questions

1. Other than the inability to talk, what was challenging about this activity?
2. What worked well? What didn't?
3. Listener and communicator, what feedback can each of you provide from your experience?
4. Is our communication always as effective as it could be?
5. What are some barriers to effective communication? How can we overcome these barriers?

The Rest of the Story

Group Size

Any

Materials

None

Time

5 to 10 minutes

Procedure

Have the team form smaller groups of four or five. Each person explains the significance of something he or she is wearing or has on his or her person (maybe in a wallet or pocket).

Start the team off in the right direction by using yourself as an example, saying something like:

> *The necklace I am wearing was made by my niece when she was eight years old. We spent the day together making pendants by wrapping silver wire around polished rocks. For me, it's a great memory of a fun day with my niece.*

Tips

Even if some team members may not be wearing any accessories (watches, rings, etc.), they can tell the story behind the shirt or shoes they have on.

Discussion Questions

1. How did it feel to divulge personal information?

2. What impact does this have on your level of trust and comfort with your team?

3. What are some other ways to build a comfort zone within our teams?

4. What are some ways we can build the level of trust within our team?

Snap, Clap, Tap

Group Size

Up to 20

Materials

Large Lego or Duplo blocks (10 per four or five players); blindfolds; painter's tape, masking tape, or rope; pads or paper; written instructions (as directed)

Time

20 to 30 minutes

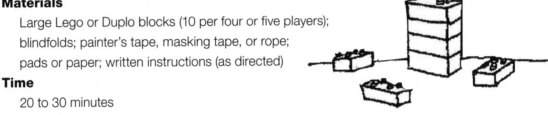

Procedure

Create a boundary for this activity by either taping or roping off a large circle on the ground. The group will build up to four 10-block structures (one per every four or five players). The circle needs to be big enough for two builders per structure to crawl around easily—up to eight people may be moving around inside the circle during the activity.

Split the group into smaller teams of four or five people. Now have each team create their structure out of 10 blocks. Have each team place their structure on a pad (or paper) on the floor within the boundary of the circle.

Now it's time to ask each member of the small teams to take on a role: builder or director. Each team needs two builders and two or three directors. Two blindfolded team members, the builders, will have to re-create the team's structure and place them exactly as they are on the pads. The directors—the sighted team members—will assist them in this endeavor.

Tell the players that once the blindfolds go on, you will disassemble and scatter the blocks throughout the playing area (the large circle on the ground). Give teams time to come up with a strategy. When everyone is ready, the blindfolds go on, and you—the facilitator—take apart the structures and scatter the pieces.

While this is being done, all the directors—the sighted players—need to get the following directions *in writing* so the builders remain unaware of the change:

> *Directors, starting* now: *no talking. The only* way you may communicate with your blindfolded team members is through nonverbal signals: clapping, tapping, stomping your feet, snapping your fingers, and so on.

From that moment on, no talking is allowed. Blindfolded players have to figure out what is going on and how to get the information they need to get the structures rebuilt.

Tips

This activity can be frustrating because the team has planned a strategy based on rules that change midway through the activity. It is best to use this with a team that needs a challenge or is going through changes in the workplace.

Assign two team members the role of "observers" to get some valuable feedback during the discussion.

Discussion Questions

1. How did you feel when the rules changed?

2. What did you have to do to achieve success?

3. How did you overcome any frustration you had?

4. Who ended up taking a lead role in the activity?

Team Tune-Up

OBJECTIVES
- To identify some of the interpersonal challenges that may negatively impact the team
- To brainstorm solutions to interpersonal challenges

Group Size
   Any
Materials
   One Team Tune-Up form (provided) for each person
Time
   15 to 20 minutes

Procedure
Pass out the Team Tune-Up form that follows to each team member. Allow between 5 and 10 minutes to complete the form individually.

Either debrief at that point or continue into a problem-solving phase by breaking the participants into four teams—each team taking one of the questions and brainstorming solutions. Then after the brainstorming session, have the teams present their ideas.

Discussion Questions
1. As you reviewed these items, did it seem like our team is an effective team?
2. How can we resolve some of the interpersonal issues that may be present?
3. How could we build in a tune-up on a regular basis?

Team Tune-Up

1. How do you feel we are doing overall? Where do we need to focus our attention?

2. How well are we working together? Why or why not? How could we be helping each other more?

3. What interpersonal issues do you see among our staff members? What is the nature of these issues?

4. What problems, if any, do you see with our operating processes, communication, decision-making, conflict resolution, and so on?

6
Creativity

Happiness lies in the joy of achievement and the thrill of creative effort.

—Franklin D. Roosevelt

Charades Relay

Group Size

Any

Materials

Charades Relay Words list (provided)

Time

15 to 20 minutes

Procedure

As the name suggests, this is a charades competition where teams "race the clock" to see how fast they can go through a list of items.

Divide the group into two or more teams of five to eight participants. Have the teams spread out so they can't hear any other team's answers. Explain to the team that all of the items on the list fall under three categories: small appliances, super heroes, and fast food items.

Each team sends one person to you—the facilitator. Whisper the first word to each person, and have the person go back to his or her team—make sure they leave at the same time—it's a race, after all. When a team guesses the word the person has acted out, someone new from the team runs up to you—the facilitator—to give the answer. If the answer is correct, you whisper to that person the next word from the list. Everyone on the team has to take a turn before anyone can come up a second time.

You can make up your own funny categories (three categories is a good number) or use the provided form.

Discussion Questions

1. Were any of you outside your comfort zones during this activity? What was that experience like for you? What helped you take that risk?

2. What impact does this have on your level of trust and comfort with your team?

3. What are some other ways to build a comfort zone within our teams?

Charades Relay Words

Use this list to track your team's progress throughout the activity

Categories: Super Heroes, Fast Food Items, Small Appliances

1. **Spiderman**
2. **Remote control**
3. **Curly fries**
4. **Defibrillator**
5. **Wonder Woman**
6. **Dishwasher**
7. **Superman**
8. **Happy Meal**
9. **Fruit juicer**
10. **Curling iron**
11. **Underdog**
12. **Onion rings**
13. **Pepperoni pizza**
14. **Batman**
15. **Captain America**
16. **Toaster**
17. **Incredible Hulk**
18. **McNuggets**
19. **Blender**
20. **Subway sandwich**

How We "C" Our Team

OBJECTIVES
- To focus on what it takes to be an effective team
- To recognize the strengths and challenges of the team

Group Size

Any

Materials

Copies of the "*C*—We're a Team!" form
(provided) for each participant

Time

15 minutes

oMMuniċation
oMMon Goals
oMpassion
onsistency
oMMitment

Procedure

Pass out copies of the "*C*—We're a Team!" form.

Ask the team members to think about all the ingredients necessary for an effective team. Then ask them to focus only on those that begin with the letter *C*. For example, the words *communication*, *compassion*, and *caring* will likely be mentioned.

Working together in groups of three or four, see how many *C* words they can come up with. Once they have their lists, have the groups identify what two *C*s they see as the team's strengths and the two *C*s the team needs to work on. Give them time to problem-solve ways to overcome the two challenging *C*s.

After allowing 7 to 10 minutes for problem solving, debrief the activity.

Notes

Some of the *C*s your teams may come up with:

- Communication
- Caring
- Consistency
- Commitment to the team

- Common goals
- Consensus
- Consideration
- Confidence
- Courtesy

Discussion Questions

1. Did you find that the help of your team members increased the number of words you identified?

2. By focusing on only one letter, do you feel that you have most of the critical components? What components are missing?

3. What are your team's strengths? Challenges? What can we do to overcome the challenges?

4. What did your team decide was the most important *C*? Was it difficult to get consensus? Why or why not?

C–We're a Team!

What does it take to be an effective team? Considering the traits necessary, how many can you come up with that start with the letter *C*?

C_____   C_____

C_____   C_____

C_____   C_____

C_____   C_____

C_____   C_____

C_____   C_____

What are the team's strengths?

C_____

C_____

What are the team's challenges?

C_____

C_____

How can the team overcome these challenges?

C_____

C_____

Kaizen

Group Size

Any

Materials

The *Kaizen* cards (provided) for each team

Time

10 to 15 minutes

Procedure

Kaizen is the Japanese word for "the continuous improvement of current processes." *Kaizen* derives from the words *kai*, meaning "change," and *zen*, meaning "good."

Form teams of four to six participants. Give one *Kaizen* card to each team. Their task is to come up with as many practical ideas and ways to improve that particular area as they can.

After 7 to 10 minutes, ask each team to present their *Kaizen* ideas to the group and explain how the ideas could be used in their (or any) organization.

Discussion Questions

1. Have you ever taken the time to do this before? Why or why not?

2. What are some benefits of this type of activity? What are some challenges?

3. How could you suggest some of your ideas to the company?

Kaizen

Copy and cut out the following cards to hand out to your team.

Communication	Marketing
Customer Relations	Productivity
Teamwork	Company Image
Motivation	E-mail Practices
Work-Life Balance	Organization Skills
Reducing Costs	Reducing Errors
Safety	Diversity

Rock Stars

OBJECTIVES
- To stretch comfort zones by taking a risk
- To get to know each other better
- To tap into our team's creativity

Group Size

Up to 30

Materials

Paper and pens for groups who want to script their performance

Time

20 to 30 minutes

Procedure

Split the large team into smaller groups of four to six participants. For the right energy and level of enthusiasm, you will want a big enough group so that you have at least three performances.

Ask the participants to think of the first concert they ever attended. Have each person think of a song from that concert and come up with a line from the song. Their group will then put all the lines together and come up with a medley, along with some awesome choreography (a routine or dance) that they will present to the whole team.

Make sure there is enough space available so the groups can spread out and practice. After 10 or 15 minutes, gather everyone together for the performances. Each group has 2 minutes to perform their act.

Tips

Your enthusiasm will get them excited about taking this risk. Tell the team, "If you can do this, you can do anything!"

Variations

Have the audience guess which line came from which team member to see how well they know each other.

Discussion Questions

1. In what way did this activity stretch your comfort zones?

2. What are some benefits of this type of activity? What are some challenges?

3. What are some other ways we can tap into each other's experiences to generate creativity in our team?

Tres Amigos

Group Size

Up to 20 in each circle—with large groups, several circles could play simultaneously.

Materials

None

Time

10 to 15 minutes

Procedure

Have the team make a circle with one person in the center (the facilitator could start in the middle to get the activity going). The goal of the game is to avoid being "It" (the person in the middle of the circle).

Here's how to play: You'll be using the list of possible formations that follows. The person who is It points to a person on the circle and says, for instance, "Elephant, one, two, three!" While the person who is It is counting, the person who was pointed at (Point person) and the persons on both sides of him or her have to coordinate their actions to make an elephant formation.

If any of the three people do not correctly respond in the three-second time period, he or she takes the center spot (the person who is It is judge and jury and can count anyone out for any reason).

- Elephant: Point person is the trunk, side people are big, floppy ears.
- Cow: Point person locks his or her fingers and turns them upside down so that the thumbs point down, forming udders; side people each grab a thumb to milk the cow.

- Palm tree: Point person is the palm tree—arms straight up, palms up—side people dance the hula.
- Nascar: Point person drives the car; side people jump in the backseat and wave to the fans.
- Jell-O: Point person wobbles like Jell-O; side people hold their arms out, forming a bowl.

Variations

A great way to get a team involved and get the creative juices flowing is to have the team make up their own formations. Give them an example so they understand the parameters—namely, a specific role for the Point person and different, specific roles for the people to the right and left of the Point person. You could even have them throw in a sound effect to go along with their formations.

Then have teams of three come up with one or two three-person configurations to teach the rest of the group. Use their ideas for the activity (a total of six or seven formations is usually the right amount of challenge).

Tips

Figure out how you want each formation to look, and make sure the expectations are clear to the team—that way you can call someone out if he or she messes it up.

Use this after lunch to regroup the team and get them back into training mode—some great energy is bound to result.

Discussion Questions

1. What was challenging about the activity? What was fun?
2. How are we creative in the workplace? How can we more easily tap into our team's creativity?
3. What are some ways we are required to come together like this in the workplace?
4. What are some things to keep in mind to work together efficiently and effectively?

Wide Open Space

Group Size

Up to 50

Materials

Flip-chart paper, painter's tape, markers

Time

20 to 30 minutes

Procedure

The basic premise of this activity is that all of us together are smarter than any one of us alone. This process has been successfully used to capture the experience and expertise of a group. It's a great way to show that learning is not a spectator sport.

Here's how it works: Anyone who would like to have a discussion or "airtime" on any topic related to the subject of the meeting is encouraged to do so. One individual (who becomes the topic's facilitator) picks up a sheet of flip-chart paper and writes out the topic in large letters. For example, if the meeting concerns time management, the topics could include "How to Get Organized," "Overcome Procrastination," and "Controlling Interruptions." The topic is announced to the group, and the individual gives a quick one-minute overview of what might be addressed during the discussion time. The topic is then posted on a wall with the facilitator standing next to it.

After everyone has had a chance to identify a topic (if they so choose), the group is asked to move around the room to visit the topic(s) they are most interested in or may have a question about.

There are no "rules," but these suggestions may be helpful:

- Whoever comes to a topic is the right person.
- Whatever happens is the right thing to happen.
- Stay in any one area (topic) for as long or as short a time as you so desire (you vote with your feet).
- After a given time, the facilitator gives a brief recap or report of what transpired at his or her station.

Tips
For a group of 30 participants, four topics is a good number. On average, look for about seven or eight team members per discussion topic. As a facilitator, you may want to have some topic ideas ready to jump-start the process.

Discussion Questions
The discussion will be based upon the topics chosen.

7

Mental Challenges

One's mind, once stretched by a new idea, never regains its original dimension.

—Oliver Wendell Holmes

Brain Strain I

OBJECTIVES

- To challenge ourselves by stretching our minds
- To consider other perspectives when problem solving
- To learn from each other

Group Size

Any

Materials

Copies of the Brain Strain I handout (provided) for each participant

Time

10 to 15 minutes

Procedure

Copy and pass out the Brain Strain I handout to each team member. Give them a few minutes to work on the questions individually, and then allow them to work in groups of four to six. After five minutes, go over the answers and the discussion questions.

Discussion Questions

1. What happened when you worked together to answer the questions?
2. Did everyone have the same perspective?
3. What were you able to learn from your teammates?
4. How does this apply to difficult tasks at work?

Brain Strain I

1. In the nursery rhyme "Sing a Song of Sixpence," how many bluebirds were baked in the pie?

2. What is the absolute last thing both men and women take off before getting into bed?

3. What 10-letter word, beginning with *T* and ending with *R*, can be typed by using only the top row of letters on a typewriter?

4. How should you pronounce the second day of the week, *Tee-use-day*, *Choose-day*, or *Twos-dee* (circle the correct pronunciation)?

5. If today is Sunday, what is the day that follows the day that comes after the day that comes before the day before yesterday?

6. Which word does not belong, and why?

noon   peep   radar   racecar   worm   level

7. In the following string of letters, can you cross out all the unnecessary letters so a logical sentence remains?

ALALTLHOEGUICNANL

ESCEENSTSEANRCYEL

REETMTAEIRSNS

8. This equation is obviously wrong. How can it be corrected without changing it?

XI + I = X

9. If a billion follows a million and a trillion follows a billion, what number follows a trillion?

10. What letters of the alphabet can be seen in this figure?

Brain Strain I Answers

1. None, they were blackbirds

2. Their feet off the floor

3. Typewriter

4. It should be pronounced as "Monday."

5. Saturday. Rearrange the sentence and it's easy: If today is Sunday, what day precedes the day before yesterday? Thursday. Then what is the day that follows the day that comes after (Thursday)? Saturday.

6. Worm. It's the only word that is not the same when spelled backward.

7. Cross out all the letters that spell *ALL THE UNNECESSARY LETTERS* and the remaining letters will spell *A LOGICAL SENTENCE REMAINS*.

8. Turn it upside down. Now it reads: 10 = 1 + 9.

9. One trillion and one

10. T, L, V, I, E, F, A, H

Brain Strain II

Group Size

Any

Materials

Copies of the Brain Strain II handout
(provided) for each participant

Time

10 to 15 minutes

Procedure

Copy and pass out the Brain Strain II handout to each team member. Give them a few minutes to work on the questions individually, and then allow them to work in teams of four to six. After five minutes, go over the answers and the discussion questions.

Discussion Questions

1. What was challenging for you? What, if anything, made your job easier?
2. What difference did it make to work with your team?
3. How can we apply this to the challenges we face in the workplace?
4. What does this tell us about teamwork?

Brain Strain II

Work with your team to decipher the hidden meaning of each box.

1. Ban ana	**2.** rider	**3.** g e s g	**4.** $$\frac{0}{\text{Dr.Ph.D.BA.}}$$
5. Mce Mce Mce	**6.** sideside	**7.** Nafish Nafish	**8.** John + MMM
9. known **FACT**	**10.** **DEAL**	**11.** B B U U R R N N	**12.** Me quit
13. BJAOCKX	**14.** RUNNING MT	**15.** FUNNY FUNNY WORDS WORDS WORDS WORDS	**16.** POIKKKKNT

Brain Strain II Answers

1. banana split

2. low rider

3. scrambled eggs

4. 3 degrees below zero

5. three blind mice (three mice with no "*I*'s")

6. side by side

7. tuna fish

8. John Adams

9. little known fact

10. big deal

11. side burns

12. quit following me

13. jack-in-the-box

14. running on empty

15. too funny for words

16. case in point

Brain Strain Classic

OBJECTIVES

- To consider different perspectives when problem solving
- To experience the benefits of team problem solving
- To build on each other's knowledge and information

Group Size

Any

Materials

Copies of the provided Brain Strain Classic handout (provided) for each participant

Time

10 to 15 minutes

Procedure

Copy and pass out the Brain Strain Classic handout to each participant. Give individuals a few minutes to consider each question and figure out the answer. Then have them work in groups of three to five participants to discuss their answers and as a team discover more accurate answers. After five minutes, go over the answers and the discussion questions.

Discussion Questions

1. What was more effective in problem solving: working individually or as a team?
2. What was different?
3. What were you able to learn from your teammates?
4. How can we apply this experience to the workplace?

Brain Strain Classic

1. Connect all nine dots with four straight lines without lifting the pen or pencil off the paper.

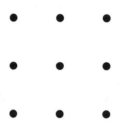

2. How many pieces or segments can you get from this circle using four straight lines?

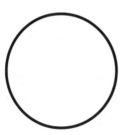

3. How many squares do you see?

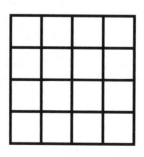

4. Shown is the Roman numeral 7. By adding only a single line, turn it into an 8.

VII

5. Here is the Roman numeral 9. By adding only a single line, turn it into a 6.

IX

6. What is half of 12? How many different answers can you find?

Brain Strain Classic Answers

1. Connect all nine dots with four straight lines without lifting the pen or pencil off the paper.

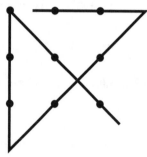

2. How many pieces or segments can you get from this circle using four straight lines? *11 pieces*

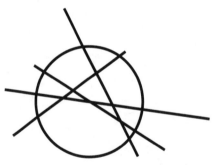

3. How many squares do you see? *30 squares: 16 small, 9 medium, 4 large, 1 big square*

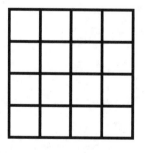

4. Shown is the Roman numeral 7. By adding only a single line, turn it into an 8.

VII**I**

5. Here is the Roman numeral 9. By adding only a single line, turn it into a 6.

SIX

(Did the previous questions make this more difficult? Why?)

6. What is half of 12? How many different answers can you find? *1, 2, 6, twe, lve (twelve)* . . .

Common Cents

Group Size

Any size; break large teams into smaller groups of six

Materials

20 pennies (or similar) for every two participants

Time

20 minutes

Procedure

This is a great game for groups of six or fewer. Each group needs 20 pennies. Break the group into two teams of three to play the game.

The game is played in two phases.

Phase One: Give the teams the following rules, and invite them to play three rounds, resulting in a best-of-three winner.

Common Cents Rules

Toss out 20 pennies. Teams take turns picking up the pennies. Each team can take one, two, or three pennies on their turn. Whichever team picks up the last penny wins the round.

Phase Two: Now add the information: "There is a strategy that ensures a 'win' every time. See if you can discover this strategy. Play three rounds to test your theory."

Ask for examples of "winning" strategies.

Tips
You can use 20 of any small object—candy, paper clips, assorted coins, and so on.

Solution
Always have the other team go first. When it's your team's turn, take whatever number of pennies you need so that the sum of each round is four. (For example, if the other person takes one, then you take three.) Follow this strategy to win every time. (They may find other solutions, which will add to the discussion.)

Discussion Questions
1. What was different about the two phases of play?

2. When searching for the solution to win every time, did you collaborate with the other half of your team? Why or why not?

3. How can we apply this experience when working with others?

4. In what ways does internal competition affect our work teams?

8

Problem Solving

In the middle of difficulty lies opportunity.

—Albert Einstein

Car Pool

OBJECTIVES

- To improve communication within the team
- To listen effectively to one another

Group Size

Up to 12

Materials

Car Pool Instructions, Car Pool Clue Cards, Car Pool Solution Cards (all provided)

Time

20 to 25 minutes

Procedure

Copy and cut out one set of clue cards and solution cards for each team. Divide the clue cards so each person gets approximately the same number of clues, and have them keep their clues facedown until they get the instructions. Give someone from the team the instructions to read aloud.

After the instructions are read, the team turns over their clues and gets started. The facilitator can either hand out the solution cards to make it easier to keep track of the possible solutions or require players to figure out the puzzle without the solution cards, which makes the game more challenging.

Variations

This chapter contains three similar problem-solving games (Car Pool, Like Clockwork, To the Dogs). The discussion questions for these three games can be interchanged to suit your purposes.

Tips

Split large groups into smaller teams of 7 to 10, and give them each a different problem-solving game (i.e., Car Pool, Like Clockwork, and To the Dogs).

Discussion Questions

1. Who made suggestions for completing the activity?

2. Were all these suggestions heard? Why or why not?

3. How did it feel to be heard when you made a suggestion?

4. What interfered with your ability to listen to others?

5. Why was it important to hear everyone's information?

6. How did you organize your information?

7. Was a leader required?

Car Pool Instructions

Robert, Erin, Zach, Kristen, and Ryan are friends who live in the same neighborhood and carpool to work together. They are all outdoor enthusiasts, with five different pastimes, five different types of vehicles, and five different professions. Your job is to figure out each person's pastime, vehicle, and profession.

You may share the information you have with the other members of your team, but you may not show anyone your cards at any time.

Good luck!

Car Pool Clue Cards

Copy and cut out the following cards to hand out to your team.

The mountain biker drives a silver minivan.	**Kristen is a rock climber.**
The musician does not drive a black truck.	**The hiker is not a musician.**
The engineer does not drive a silver minivan.	**The runner drives a red SUV.**
Kristen is not an engineer.	**The musician is not a rock climber.**
Robert is not an architect.	**The architect does not drive a blue jeep.**
Ryan is a partner at his firm.	**The teacher drives a black truck.**
The mountain biker is not a teacher.	**Zach is not a runner.**
The golfer drives a black truck.	**The golfer's name is not Robert.**
Ryan does not like to hike.	**Kristen is not a musician.**
Erin drives a blue jeep.	**The mountain biker is not a lawyer.**
The rock climber does not drive a blue jeep.	**Robert does not drive a red SUV.**
The lawyer does not drive a green hybrid.	

Car Pool Solution Cards

Copy and cut out the following cards to hand out to your team.

Solution Cards: Names

Robert	Erin
Zach	Kristen
Ryan	

Solution Cards: Vehicles

Black truck	Blue jeep
Green hybrid	Red SUV
Silver minivan	

Solution Cards: Pastimes

Golfer	Hiker
Mountain biker	Rock climber
Runner	

Solution Cards: Professions

Architect	Engineer
Lawyer	Musician
Teacher	

Car Pool Solution

Robert: mountain biker, musician, silver minivan

Erin: hiker, engineer, blue jeep

Zach: golfer, teacher, black truck

Kristen: rock climber, architect, green hybrid

Ryan: runner, lawyer, red SUV

Card Shark

OBJECTIVES
- To improve communication within the team
- To share information for effective problem solving
- To overcome the frustration of working through a challenging task

Group Size
Up to 10

Materials
Card Shark Instructions, Card Shark diagram handout, Card Shark Clue Cards (all provided)

Time
20 to 30 minutes

Procedure
Make copies of the instructions and diagram for each team of five to ten participants. Make one set of the clue cards for each team. Divide the clue cards so each person gets approximately the same number of clues, and have them keep their clues facedown until they get the instructions.

Have someone from the team read the instructions. The team then turns over their clues and gets started. They can use the Card Shark diagram handout to organize their information.

Tips
Split a larger group into smaller teams of 5 to 10, and let each team figure it out. While this activity may appear to be similar to Car Pool, Like Clockwork, and To the Dogs, it is far more challenging and can be frustrating.

Discussion Questions

1. How well did you listen?

2. Did you prevent yourself from listening well? How?

3. Did you listen in the same manner for this activity as you normally listen? If not, what was different?

4. How effectively did the team handle frustrations?

5. What could you have done to handle this challenge more effectively?

6. What ideas can we take from this experience to help us solve difficult problems as a team?

Card Shark Instructions

On the handout diagram you see there are 13 cards shown facedown. The Ace is considered high. Based on your clues, what are the numbers, suits, and positions of the 13 cards?

You may share the information you have with the other members of your team, but you may not show anyone your cards at any time.

Good luck!

Card Shark

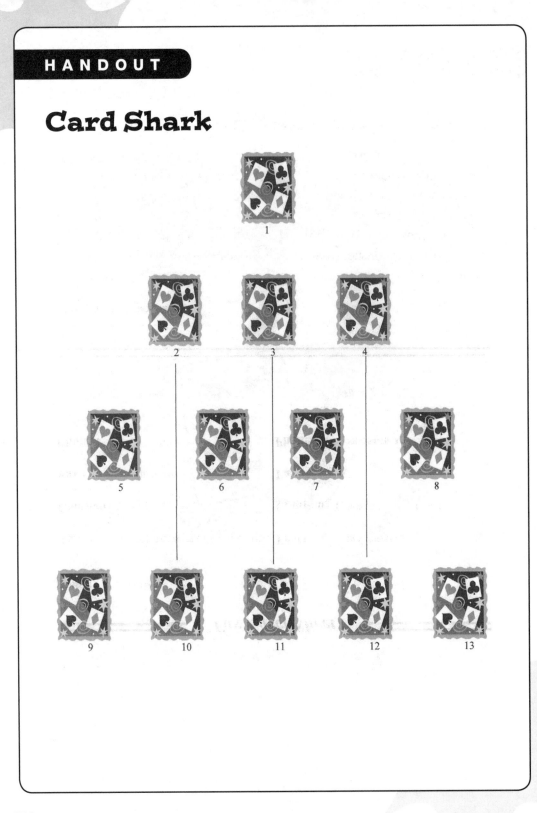

Card Shark Clue Cards

Copy and cut out the following cards to hand out to your team.

At least three cards of each suit are represented.	**Card 5 ranks one lower than card 9.**
There is exactly one card of each denomination in the layout.	**Card 5 ranks one higher than card 2.**
Each suit is represented by just one of the four top-ranking cards (Jack to Ace).	**Card 8 is the same color as card 4.**
The Queen is in a direct line above the 4 of clubs.	**Card 8 and card 4 are not the same suit.**
The highest diamond is in the row directly above the highest spade.	**Card 6 is the same color as card 11.**
The first card and the last card are the same suit.	**Card 6 and card 11 are not the same suit.**
The Jack of clubs is diagonally immediately below and to the right of a heart.	**Card 10 is a face card.**
Card 12 is the 2 of the same suit as card 7.	**Card 1 (top card) is a 3 of clubs.**
One of the hearts is immediately to the left of a spade.	**The 6 in row three has a diamond on each side of it.**
The 7 is farther to the right than the 8 in the same row.	

Card Shark Solution

1. 3 of clubs

2. 8 of spades

3. Queen of hearts

4. 7 of diamonds

5. 9 of diamonds

6. 6 of spades

7. Ace of diamonds

8. 5 of hearts

9. 10 of hearts

10. King of spades

11. 4 of clubs

12. 2 of diamonds

13. Jack of clubs

Catch and Release

Group Size

Any

Materials

One bouncy ball or tennis ball for each team member

Time

10 minutes

Procedure

Split any large groups into smaller teams of six or seven, and have them form a circle. Each person gets a ball.

The rule is that as soon as anyone catches a ball thrown to him or her by a team member, that person must *immediately* toss it to someone else on the team (all balls must be tossed, not handed). No one should ever be holding a ball—everyone is either tossing, catching, or both—while the game is being played. If a ball is dropped, simply pick it up and return it to play.

Ask a volunteer from each team to count how many balls get dropped during the activity. They have one minute on the clock after you say, "Go!"

Ask each team how many balls were dropped. You can score the teams individually or add the totals together for a group score.

Now let them know they will have a chance to improve their score. For the second round, the same rules apply, except that the team members will have some planning time. Give them about a minute or two. When it seems like all the teams are ready, give them another minute—then say, "Go!"

Ask each team how many balls were dropped during this round.

Discussion Questions

1. Why the big difference (there usually is a difference) between the two rounds?

2. What strategies were effective?

3. Do we always take the time to plan? Why or why not?

4. Why is it important to take time to plan, even when things are crazy or moving quickly?

Like Clockwork

Group Size

Up to 12

Materials

Like Clockwork Instructions, Like Clockwork Clue Cards, Like Clockwork Solution Cards (all provided)

Time

20 to 25 minutes

Procedure

Copy and cut out the one set of clue cards and solution cards for each team. Divide the clue cards so each person gets approximately the same number of clues, and have them keep the clues facedown until they get the instructions.

Have someone from the team read the instructions. The team then turns over their clues and gets started. You can hand out the solution cards to make it easier to keep track of the solution or require them to figure it out without the solution cards, which is more challenging.

Variations

This book contains three similar problem-solving games (Car Pool, Like Clockwork, To the Dogs). The discussion questions for these three games can be interchanged to suit your purposes.

Tips

Split large groups into smaller teams of 7 to 10, and give them each a different problem-solving game (Car Pool, Like Clockwork, To the Dogs).

Discussion Questions

1. How well did you listen?

2. How did you organize your information?

3. How could your process have been more effective?

4. Was a leader required?

5. Why was it important to hear everyone's information?

6. What problem-solving techniques can we take from this experience?

Like Clockwork Instructions

The barista has been working at the same coffee shop for years. She loves her job because she has lots of regular customers. In fact, five of her customers are like clockwork—they always order the same thing at the same time every morning on their way to work. When it comes to the five predictable customers— Mike, Jackie, Todd, Catherine, and Alexander—your job is to determine what time they come in, what drink they order, and what they purchase along with their morning beverage.

You may share the information you have with the other members of your group, but you may not show anyone your cards at any time.

Good luck!

Like Clockwork Clue Cards

Copy and cut out the following cards to hand out to your team.

The customer who buys the hot cocoa comes in to the shop right after Catherine.	**Todd comes in at 8:25.**
The hot cocoa drinker always buys the morning paper.	**Catherine is not a "dunker."**
Mike eats cereal at home before heading out for the day.	**Todd never eats breakfast.**
Jackie comes in earlier than the person who buys the muffin.	**The tea drinker gets the morning news online.**
Alexander orders his green.	**The coffee drinker does not like muffins.**
The mocha drinker arrives at exactly 8:15 every morning.	**The latte drinker gets a donut.**

The person who eats the croissant does not drink a mocha.

The hot cocoa drinker is not the last customer.

The donut is purchased at 8:20.

Mike orders his drink without whipped cream.

The coffee drinker does not ever eat donuts.

Mike and Todd work together.

Catherine is not the first customer.

Catherine orders her drink with skim milk.

Alexander eats breakfast every day.

The latte drinker does not eat a croissant.

The person with minty-fresh breath is not named Todd.

Jackie doesn't read the paper.

Like Clockwork Solution Cards

Copy and cut out the following cards to hand out to your team.

Solution Cards: Names

Jackie	Mike
Catherine	Todd
Alexander	

Solution Cards: Times

8:10	8:25
8:15	8:30
8:20	

Solution Cards: Beverages

Mocha	Latte
Hot cocoa	Tea
Coffee	

Solution Cards: Purchases

Newspaper	Croissant
Mints	Donut
Muffin	

Like Clockwork Solution

8:10: Jackie, coffee, croissant

8:15: Mike, mocha, mints

8:20: Catherine, latte, donut

8:25: Todd, hot cocoa, newspaper

8:30: Alexander, tea, muffin

SCOT (SWOT) Analysis

Group Size

Any

Materials

Copies of the SCOT Analysis form (provided) for each person

Time

15 to 20 minutes

Procedure

Copy and pass out the SCOT (Strengths, Challenges, Opportunities, and Threats) Analysis form. Many participants may be familiar with the SWOT (Strengths, Weaknesses, Opportunities, and Threats) concept. This exercise focuses on "Challenges" rather than "Weaknesses."

Ask the team members to first fill out this form individually, as it applies to their particular situation. After allowing five to seven minutes for this, have them form small discussion groups of four to six to discuss the points identified.

Ask for volunteers to explain why they filled out the form as they did.

Discussion Questions

1. As you looked at this form, was it fairly easy to "fill in the blanks"?

2. Does your organization have a healthy attitude toward teamwork?

3. What are some of the interpersonal issues this form brings out?

4. How could your challenges be resolved?

SCOT Analysis

Strengths	Challenges
Opportunities	**Threats**

Ship, Captain, and Crew

OBJECTIVES

- To emphasize that every team member—regardless of title or position—plays an integral part in the team's overall effectiveness
- To consider other perspectives, and keep an open mind

Group Size

Any

Materials

Ship, Captain, and Crew form (provided) for each person

Time

10 to 15 minutes

Procedure

Ask the team to name all the different positions, jobs, or roles of the people you would find on a cruise ship. Write them on a flip chart as they come up with their answers. Then ask, "Who is the most important?"

Pass out copies of the Ship, Captain, and Crew form. Ask team members to identify who on that ship is the most important person or plays the most critical role. Then have them write down their answer along with the reason for their choice.

Tips

Before they start reporting, acknowledge that at first glance, it might seem obvious that the captain of the ship is the most important person. But ask them to consider that other roles may be just as—or even more—important.

Discussion Questions

1. What were your initial responses? (for example, captain, engineer, house-keeper, social director, chef, etc.)

2. In your discussion with your team, did you find it easy to convince them of your selection? Why or why not?

3. Did any of you change your mind? What convinced you to do so?

4. Is it always important to reach consensus within a team? Why or why not?

5. What are some similar situations where it benefits the team to achieve consensus?

6. In your own work situation, how can you help others realize that even the seemingly most menial job at the company still makes significant contributions?

Ship, Captain, and Crew

On a cruise ship, who—or which position—is the *most* important?

My response: _____

Why?

_____

_____

_____

_____

Team Consensus:

_____

_____

_____

_____

Why?

_____

_____

_____

_____

Each team will report on their discussion and will defend their decision.

To the Dogs

Group Size

Up to 12

Materials

To the Dogs Instructions, To the Dogs Clue Cards, To the Dogs Solution Cards (all provided)

Time

20 to 25 minutes

Procedure

Copy and cut out one set of clue cards and the solution cards for each team. Divide the clue cards so each person gets approximately the same number of clues, and have them keep the clues facedown until they get the instructions.

Ask someone from the team to read the instructions. The team then turns over their clues and gets to work. You can hand out the solution cards to make it easier to keep track of the solution or require them to figure it out without the cards, which is more challenging.

Variations

This book contains three similar problem-solving games (Car Pool, Like Clockwork, To the Dogs). The discussion questions for these three games can be interchanged to suit your purposes.

Tips

Split large groups into smaller teams of 7 to 10, and give them each a different problem-solving game (Car Pool, Like Clockwork, To the Dogs).

Discussion Questions

1. What process did you use to figure out your solution?

2. What could you have done differently?

3. What is challenging about team problem solving?

4. What is beneficial about working together to solve problems?

5. How can we use this experience to problem solve more effectively in the workplace?

To the Dogs Instructions

The women who work at AnyCo are all avid dog lovers. In fact, they have a standing "play date" every week. The five women and their dogs, Oscar, Chester, Gonzo, Zeus, and Brooks, meet every Saturday morning at the dog park. The dogs get along so well, that even though they each bring their own favorite toy to the park, they have no problem sharing with one another. Toys are scattered everywhere as they run and play together. When it's time to leave, it can get confusing—who goes home with which owner and what toy?

Your job is to figure out each dog's owner, breed, and favorite toy. You may verbally share your information with your team, but you may not show anyone your cards at any time.

Good luck!

To the Dogs Clue Cards

Copy and cut out the following cards to hand out to your team.

Karen throws the tennis ball to her dog.	**Karen does not have a Lab.**
The poodle does not chase golf balls.	**Michelle tosses a golf ball to her dog.**
The collie does not chase tennis balls.	**Brooks does not belong to Alice.**
Chester is not a collie.	**Oscar catches his Frisbee in midair.**
Gonzo is not a golden retriever.	**Karen does not own the mutt.**
The golden retriever does not like Frisbees.	**Zeus is not the name of Janet's dog.**
Alice does not have a poodle.	**The Lab loves to run after golf balls.**

Chester belongs to Sandy.	Michelle's dog is not Gonzo.
The mutt loves his squeaky toy.	Sandy does not know how to toss a Frisbee.
The poodle does not belong to Sandy.	Chester is not a poodle.
Brooks is a lovable mutt.	The squeaky toy doesn't go home with Gonzo.
The mutt does not play with old socks.	

To the Dogs Solution Cards

Copy and cut out the following cards to hand out to your team. Each word is a separate solution card.

Solution Cards: Names

Oscar	Chester
Gonzo	Zeus
Brooks	

Solution Cards: Owners

Alice	Janet
Karen	Sandy
Michelle	

Solution Cards: Favorite Toys

Tennis ball	Squeaky toy
Old sock	Frisbee
Golf ball	

Solution Cards: Dog Breeds

Poodle	Lab
Mutt	Collie
Golden retriever	

To the Dogs Solution

Karen: Gonzo, poodle, tennis ball

Alice: Oscar, collie, Frisbee

Michelle: Zeus, lab, golf ball

Sandy: Chester, golden retriever, old sock

Janet: Brooks, mutt, squeaky toy

9

Recognition

You already have every characteristic necessary for success if you recognize, claim, develop, and use them.

—Zig Ziglar

Back Words

Group Size

Up to 20

Materials

For each participant: a stack of sticky notes (in different shapes and colors work best—they have two rows of adhesive), a piece of blank paper, a marker

Time

20 to 30 minutes

Procedure

Have participants brainstorm the qualities and characteristics of effective team members. As they are coming up with their ideas, the facilitator (or someone from the team) writes the words on a flip chart or whiteboard.

There must be the same number of qualities and characteristics as there are team members. The list could include qualities such as *good listener, productive, good communication skills, organized, good time-management skills, confident, people skills, reliable, responsive, adaptable, trustworthy, responsible, follows through, good problem-solving skills, enthusiastic, inspiring, motivating* and so on.

Give each team member a stack of sticky notes, and have them write the words from the flip chart on each sticky note (one word per note). Each person ends up with a stack of notes equal to the number of participants in the room. Now it's time to "pat each other on the back."

Encourage the team to look around the room and consider what qualities they have seen exhibited during the program and what each person contributed.

The goal now is to distribute their notes. Each person gives each of the other team members a sticky note with one of the qualities that he or she thinks pertains to that particular individual. This is done by putting the appropriate sticky note on the person's back. (Each person will end up with one extra note—perhaps this is the quality he or she contributed?)

Once all the notes are distributed, the team members can work with partners to put all their notes on a sheet of paper, which they can have as a program takeaway.

Tips

Team members may want to make a note of the qualities and skills that weren't given to them. They could then work on those skills and qualities.

Discussion Questions

1. Why is it so important to give each other positive feedback?

2. Do we always take the time to do this? How can we make it more a part of our interactions?

Thank-You Bingo

OBJECTIVES

- To consider how the other team members influenced our experience throughout the training
- To take the time to show appreciation to the other team members

Group Size

Any

Materials

Thank-You Bingo form (provided) for each team member

Time

10 to 20 minutes

Procedure

Hand out copies of the Thank-You Bingo form to everyone on the team. Give the participants a few minutes to reflect on their day and how the other team members contributed to their experience during the training.

Then have the team mingle and choose someone different to sign his or her name in each box . . . getting as many boxes signed as possible—and giving each other some well-deserved appreciation. Here are some examples of what people might say:

Cynthia, you make even the most challenging tasks enjoyable with your enthusiasm and can-do attitude, thank you! Can I get your autograph in the box that says, "Has a great attitude," because you sure do!

Paul, you showed strong leadership skills by keeping us on track and focused during the Type Cast activity after lunch. It made a big difference in our time. Thank you! Your name needs to go in the box that says, "Has good leadership skills." Would you mind signing it for me?

The challenge is to get as many signed as possible in the time given—or at least enough for a bingo.

Tips

Give them enough time to provide specifics to the person signing the square. If time is short, just have them fill out five in a row for a bingo.

Discussion Questions

1. How did it feel to take the time to show appreciation?

2. How did it feel to receive recognition from your teammates?

3. When providing appreciation, what makes it meaningful?

4. How does this impact the overall energy level and productivity of a team?

Thank-You Bingo

Take a minute to reflect on your experience today and how it was enhanced by different members of your team. As you have each team member sign the box that reflects your appreciation of him or her, take time to provide the specifics regarding your appreciation.

Made you laugh	You got to know better	Showed you a different perspective	Surprised you	Is a good communicator
Gave you a hand	Kept an open mind	Is fun to be around	Works well with others	Deserves a pat on the back
Did something amazing	Provided encouragement	Free	Made an improvement	Is a great listener
Has positive energy	Took a risk	Inspires you	Has a great attitude	Has good leadership skills
Is creative	Played a different role	Is a good problem solver	Challenged you	Taught you something new

The Tribe Has Spoken

OBJECTIVES
- To brainstorm the traits of the non-team-player and contrast them with the traits of the ultimate team player
- To become aware of counterproductive actions
- To consider what it takes to be a contributing member of the team

Group Size

Any

Materials

Copies of the Profile of a Non-Team-Player and Profile of the Ulitimate Team Player forms for each team

Time

10 to 15 minutes

Procedure

Split a large group into smaller teams of four to six people. Pass out the forms to each team. Say the following:

> *From time to time, we are all "difficult" team members; perhaps we are stressed, tired, or preoccupied—and we are not contributing according to our normal standard.*
>
> *Imagine a team member with every negative characteristic. What would that look like? What qualities and characteristics would a person consistently exhibit to get themselves "voted off" the team?*

Have the participants consider that question, brainstorm with their team, and complete the worksheet. Give the teams 5 to 10 minutes to brainstorm and complete their forms, after which you can open the discussion to the larger group.

Discussion Questions

1. What qualities and characteristics are counterproductive?

2. Have we all experienced or displayed some of these qualities? Why? What can we do about it?

3. How can this activity help us become more effective team members?

4. What are some qualities an effective team member would exhibit?

5. What is our individual responsibility to the team?

Profile of a Non-Team-Player

While answering these questions, think of the non-team-player's interactions with other team members:

1. What would the non-team-player say or fail to say?

2. What would the non-team-player do or fail to do?

3. What would the non-team-player think or fail to think?

4. What are counterproductive traits, characteristics, and qualities?

Profile of the Ultimate Team Player

While answering these questions, think of the ultimate team player's interactions with other team members:

1. What would the ultimate team player say or fail to say?

2. What would the ultimate team player do or fail to do?

3. What would the ultimate team player think or fail to think?

4. What are other productive traits, characteristics, and qualities?

Toss Me Some Feedback

Group Size

Any

Materials

Balls, beanbags, or similar tossing items; blindfolds; stopwatch; painter's or masking tape

Time

15 minutes

Procedure

Split a larger group into smaller teams of three to seven people. Each of these teams needs one blindfold and one ball.

Tape a start line and goal box for each smaller team. The goal box should be at least 15 feet from the start line; the goal boxes should be about 3 feet by 3 feet.

Each team needs a tosser, a retriever, a scorekeeper, and an assistant. Any other team members can provide feedback during rounds two and three. One point is scored for every ball the tosser gets into the goal box (the ball can roll out as long as it bounced into the goal box first). The goal is for the tosser to score as many points as possible in one minute.

Each round is one minute. The tosser is blindfolded, then stands behind the start line and tosses the ball. The retriever picks up the ball and throws it back to the assistant, who gives it to the tosser to try again. The scorekeeper adds up the successful tosses for each round.

Round one: No talking—the tossers attempt to score as many points as possible with no input or coaching from their team. Record the team score by adding up the scores from all the tossers.

Round two: The team can coach their tossers by saying either "Yeah" or "Boo"—but nothing else. Record the team score.

Round three: The team can coach their tossers by providing any helpful information. Record the team score.

Discussion Questions

1. Tossers: What was challenging, and how did you overcome?
2. Team: How did it feel to simply watch? In the workplace do we simply watch, or are we willing to help each other and accept help from others? What makes this process effective?
3. What kind of feedback is the most effective? Why?

Thank-You Notes

Group Size

Up to 30 works best

Materials

Envelopes (one for each team member), markers in assorted colors, blank sheets of paper

Time

10 to 20 minutes (spread throughout the day)

Procedure

Before the program, cut the blank paper into four equal pieces. Have enough paper so each person has at least 10 pieces to use during the day. Place assorted colored markers and the pieces of paper throughout the room. As the participants enter the training room at the beginning of the program, give each an envelope. Ask them to write their names and decorate the envelopes to personalize them. When they are done, place all envelopes in a visible place in the room.

Once everyone is present, let them know that throughout the day, they will have opportunities to express their appreciation to other members of the team. The notes can be short and simple, as well as sincere and specific. Participants can remain anonymous, or they can sign the notes. Before breaks, lunches, and prior to ending the program, give the team a few minutes to reflect on their experience and jot down a note of thanks to whomever they chose.

At the end of the day, you may choose to give them some time to read their notes before taking their envelopes with them.

Tips

This is a great activity for a one-day or multiday program. That way, team members have more experiences together to draw from and more opportunities to take the time to jot down their thoughts.

Discussion

1. Why is it important to give and receive appreciation?

2. How does it feel to receive recognition? To give recognition?

3. In what ways does the team benefit from an activity such as this one?

10

Outdoor Games

Just play. Have fun. Enjoy the game.

—Michael Jordan

Cross the Line

Group Size

Any

Materials

Painter's tape, masking tape, or rope

Time

10 to 15 minutes

Procedure

Tape a 20-foot line on the floor, or place a 20-foot rope on the ground (for a team of 20 or fewer). Have participants pair up. One partner stands on one side of the tape and the other partner on the other side of the tape.

Say the following:

When I say "Go," your goal is to get your partner on your side of the tape. On your mark, get set . . . wait! One more thing—you must do so without ever touching your partner.

Give them a "Go," and let them start negotiating.

Based on where the partners end up, you can discuss what the different outcomes look like and how they got there.

Discussion Questions

1. What various outcomes did we see?

2. Those of you who "won," that is, got your partner to come to your side of the tape, what did it take to get him or her there? What are some situations where we make concessions?

3. Do we make concessions or accept a win-lose without even considering the possibility of a win-win?

4. What does a win-win look like in this activity? How do we get there?

5. In what way does trust come into play when people are looking for a win-win?

Rescue the Mascot

OBJECTIVES

- To unify the team by working toward a common goal
- To collaborate to protect our resources
- To experience the process that takes us from a group of individuals and turns us into a team

Group Size

15 to 20 works best

Materials

A large stuffed animal (one that is difficult to conceal behind a person's back)

Time

20 to 30 minutes

Procedure

Create a 10-foot baseline and a 20-foot goal line by placing or nailing rope to the ground. The baseline needs to be about 100 feet from the goal line (see diagram). The facilitator stands just outside the baseline with the mascot (stuffed animal) placed on the ground behind him or her. The team stands at the other end of the field just behind the goal line. The object is to proceed down the field, rescue the mascot, and get the mascot back over the goal line without the facilitator knowing who has the mascot.

Once everyone is in their starting positions, the facilitator turns his or her back, counts to three, turns around to face the team, and says, "Freeze." If anyone is caught moving, the team starts over. The facilitator continues to turn his or her back and say, "1, 2, 3, freeze" as the team proceeds down the field to get their mascot.

Once the team reaches their mascot, the real challenge begins. The facilitator now has to try to get the mascot back by guessing who possesses it. (Only one person can have possession of the mascot at a time.) The facilitator tries to guess who has the mascot when he or she turns around and yells, "Freeze." If the facilitator guesses correctly, play starts again. (Whoever the facilitator guesses has to hold both arms up to prove he or she doesn't have the mascot.) The team wins when they get their mascot back over the goal without the facilitator guessing who possesses the mascot.

Teams quickly figure out they need to come together and make it difficult to guess who is holding the mascot. Every time the facilitator turns his or her back, the mascot changes possession. Remember that only one person can possess the mascot at a time. Even the players who don't have possession are fully engaged with trying to confuse the facilitator.

Tips

Count off the "1, 2, 3, freeze" using a consistent cadence to assist the team in strategizing.

For additional rounds, team members can take the place of the facilitator—they love it!

Discussion Questions

1. How did you make sure your mascot was safe?

2. How did you come up with your strategies? Did you develop better strategies as the activity went on? Why or why not?

3. How do you feel your team came together to achieve your goal?

4. What can we do to maintain this team mentality?

Rescue the Mascot Activity Diagram

The facilitator stands behind the baseline.

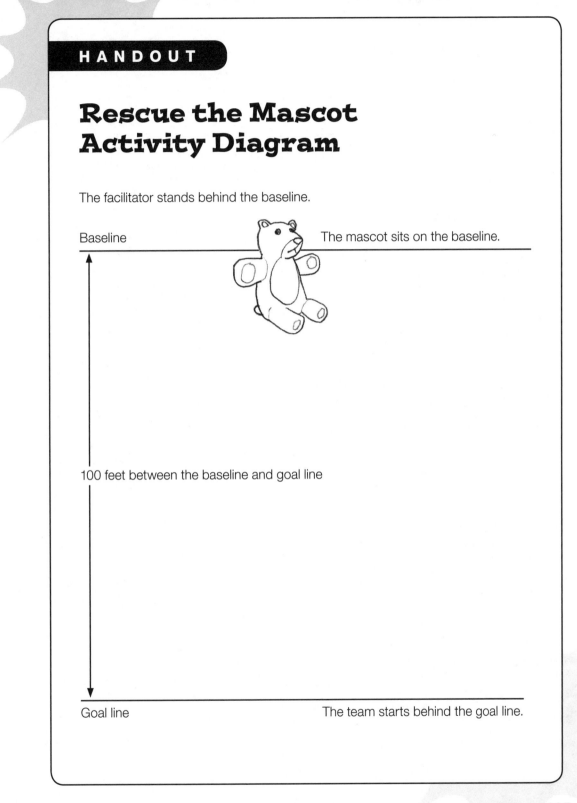

Baseline — The mascot sits on the baseline.

100 feet between the baseline and goal line

Goal line — The team starts behind the goal line.

Ringer

OBJECTIVES

- To energize the team
- To overcome challenges and solve problems together
- To develop a deeper level of trust

Group Size

Any

Materials

One hula hoop for each team of 10 to 20 participants

Time

10 to 15 minutes

Procedure

Have participants form a circle and hold hands. One team member—the "Ringer"—stands inside a hula hoop that is placed on the ground. The objective is to get the hoop from where it is on the ground to outside of the circle of people without the participants letting go of their hands.

The Ringer, who is the person standing on the ground inside the hoop, cannot move his or her feet whatsoever. The rest of the team is free to move in whatever way they choose to achieve success as long as they maintain their connection. If anyone on the team breaks a connection (stops holding hands), or if the Ringer moves his or her feet, reset the team and the hoop, and start the activity again.

Tips

You can break a larger group into smaller teams of 10 to 20 and have several teams do the activity at the same time. Provide the discussion questions to each team, and let them have their own discussion (a great way for them to take ownership of their experience).

Discussion Questions

1. How did you feel when you had to start over? Did you do anything different the second time? (You will not use this question if they were successful the first time).

2. What did it take to be successful?

3. What made it easy to trust the team?

4. What similar situations occur at work? How do we come together to achieve success?

Square Off

Group Size

10 to 20 participants

Materials

One 100-foot rope, tied with a knot; blindfolds for each team member

Time

10 to 15 minutes

Procedure

Place the rope on the ground lengthwise. One half of the team stands on one side of the rope and the other half on the other side of the rope. Have the team members bend their arms at the elbow, point at the person across from them, and say, "How you doin'?" (This demonstrates the hand position for holding the rope once the blindfolds go on.) Now that they are familiar with the hand position, pass out the blindfolds.

Have the team put their blindfolds on, and ask them to bend their arms and put their hands out in the "How you doin'?" position. The facilitator then places the rope in each team member's hands. Tell the team that once the rope is in their hands, they are to remain attached to the rope for the duration of the activity. Team members may move along the rope, but they are not to let go nor move around other team members to get a different position.

Once everyone is holding the rope, give them their objective: as a team, they need to form a square with the rope. When the team is in agreement that they have a square, they can put the rope on the ground and take off the blindfolds.

Tips

For a more challenging version, make a few twists and turns in the rope when placing it on the ground. This version takes twice as much time and is much more physical because oftentimes the team members have to step over or under the rope to create their square.

Discussion Questions

1. How did you overcome the challenge of being blindfolded?

2. What other obstacles did you face? How did you overcome them?

3. How effectively did you communicate? What would you do differently?

4. How effective is your communication in the workplace? What could you do to improve it?

5. Did anyone take a leadership role? Was a leadership role required? Why or why not?

Type Cast

Group Size

Teams of 10 to 20 work best

Materials

Paper plates or spot markers numbered 1 through 9 and all the letters of the alphabet (35 plates or spot markers in all), stopwatch, rope and nails for outdoors or painter's or masking tape for indoors

Time

25 to 30 minutes

Procedure

Split the team in half. One half stays in the playing area, and one half goes to a location that is out of view of the playing area. Tell the half going to the remote location that you will join them with some information in a few minutes.

The remaining half sets up the game. Pull out the spot markers and the tape. They need to create a large rectangle (10 feet by 20 feet is a good size) and scatter the letters and numbers throughout the inside of that rectangle. Once they are finished, tell them the following:

> You are the design half of the team. You have just designed a new keyboard. Now since this is your final prototype, all the "keys" have to remain where they are. You may spend the next five minutes familiarizing yourselves with the new keyboard you created.

(You are deliberately being vague.) Let them know you will come back to get them in a few minutes to join the other half of the team in the remote location.

Now go meet with the other half. Tell them the following,

The other half of your team is creating an improved keyboard. Your job is to test the new keyboard to see if it is more efficient than the current keyboard. First, you have to come up with a 25- to 30-character (i.e., letters, numbers, or both) phrase—for example: "With teamwork everything is more fun."

Now give them the other rules:

1. *Only one person is allowed on the keyboard at a time (inside the tape).*
2. *Any misspelling or typo results in a penalty (either a 10-second penalty per typo or starting over).*
3. *Everyone on the team (the whole team) must type in at least one number or letter by stepping on the plates.*

Once the remote half has the phrase and the rules, bring the team together in the remote location and give them time to plan—about 10 minutes. Then they all go to the keyboard to begin. Once everyone is circled around the outside of the keyboard, yell "Go" and start the stopwatch. Their first attempt establishes a baseline, after which they have two additional attempts to improve their time. (The facilitator is the official timekeeper.)

Discussion Questions

1. What communication challenges did you have to overcome?
2. What other challenges did you experience? How did you overcome them?
3. How did you get organized?
4. What are some reasons we withhold information in the workplace? What are the repercussions?
5. In what ways did trust play a factor in this activity?
6. If we did this activity again, would you do anything differently? What?
7. How does this relate to some of the challenges we face in the workplace?
8. How can you use this experience to improve similar situations at work?

Build a Word

Group Size

Up to 20

Materials

Rope; nails; 13 3 × 5 cards (write one letter of the word "COMMUNICATION" on each card); blank 3 × 5 cards; blindfolds; assorted small, soft props such as squeaky toys or bean bag animals

Time

20 to 30 minutes

Procedure

Create a boundary 10 feet wide and between 20 and 30 feet long with the rope. Create two distinct and even sides by making a rope-line across the length of the playing area. Distribute cards (letters facedown) and obstacles throughout the playing field so there is the same number of cards as team members on each side. To make it fair, make sure there is also the same number of props (obstacles) on each side.

If you have more than 13 team members, place blank cards on the playing field so there is the same number of cards as people. When distributing the letters, put all the vowels on one side, and the consonants on the other. This means one half gets six letters and one half gets seven letters; allocate blank cards to make up the difference.

Split the team in half, and have each half go to opposite sides of the playing area (on the outside of the rope). Give everyone a blindfold and the instructions:

> The goal is to collect all the cards from your half of the playing area with the ultimate goal of spelling out a word. Each side's half of the playing area is the opposite side from where you start. Everyone on the team must make a trip through the course, collect one card, and exit on the opposite side. Team members must be blindfolded before stepping into the course. If you step on an obstacle, you have to start over. Any card in your possession must then be put back down.
>
> Sighted team members can direct blindfolded team members through the course, but you can only direct from the side you are on. This means that you must direct from your starting line, but as team members end up on the other side, you can direct from that side as well. The 20- (or 30-) foot sides are off limits to team members. Only blindfolded team members can be inside the course. After the team has collected the letters, you have to spell a word.

Give the sides a couple minutes to plan, and then have both sides begin at the same time.

Create a sense of urgency by limiting the time they have to collect and spell the word. Ultimately they need to work together to spell the word, but that may not happen. They may ask if they can work with the "other team," to which you can reply, "You are one team. You can work with whomever you would like."

Tips

Choose two different colors of 3 × 5 cards for each half of the team's letters—consonants on one color, vowels on the other. Give one side one color blindfold, and the other side a different color. This creates more of a perceived competition, and it can lead to a more in-depth discussion about perceived versus actual competition. This could also lead to a discussion on what separates us in the workplace and how those separations impact the team.

After explaining the rules, have each half of the team set up the area closest to them (which will be the other half's playing field). Will they make it easy or difficult for the other half? How does this relate to the workplace?

When talking about each group, be sure to refer to them as "the other half" rather than "the other team."

Variations

If you have fewer than 13 team members, have them pick up two cards as they go through the course.

This can be played indoors if you have enough space, using tape to mark the course. One word of caution: the noise level can get pretty high when inside.

Discussion Questions

1. How was communication within your team?

2. Did you receive any help from the other half of your team? Did you offer any help to the other half? Why or why not?

3. In what ways did you have to extend trust?

4. What are some ways in which we create imaginary boundaries in the workplace?

5. What would you do differently if you had to do this activity again?

About the Authors

Founder and owner of BizTeamTools.com, Mary Scannell puts theory into practice by leading nearly 100 corporate trainings every year, throughout the United States and Canada.

After a decade of teaching hard skills, Mary branched into the interpersonal discipline of Team Building in 1999, facilitating in a wide variety of corporate and educational settings. She has trained tens of thousands of people, including a long list of *Fortune 500* clientele.

Mary's expertise in Team Building and Group Activities extends through the full gamut of the topic—from small classroom exercises to large-scale outdoor adventure events.

An active member of the National Speakers Association, Ed Scannell has given more than a thousand presentations, seminars, and workshops across the United States and internationally.

He has written or coauthored 20 books and more than 100 articles in the fields of HRD, Creativity, Team Building, and Management. He has served as ASTD's (American Society for Training and Development) National President and also as Executive Chairman for IFTDO (International Federation of Training and Development Organizations).

A past president of MPI's (Meeting Professionals International) Arizona chapter, he was elected as MPI's International President in 1990. He was named MPI's International Planner of the Year in 1995 and was inducted into the Convention Industry Council's Hall of Leaders in 2007.

Ed was elected National President of the National Speakers Association (NSA) in 1991–92 and received NSA's highest honor, the Cavett award, in 1997.

He is currently serving as the Director of the Center for Professional Development and Training in Scottsdale, Arizona.